Restoring American Freedom
A PRIMER FOR A CONSTITUTIONALIST CONGRESS

By Alan B. Jones

ISBN 978-0-9773268-6-0
Copyright 2011 by Alan B. Jones

PUBLISHED BY

Life & Liberty Publishing

P.O. BOX 638, CHELTENHAM, MD 20623

ORDERS MAY BE SENT TO:

Life & Liberty Publishing

P.O. BOX 2770, STAFFORD, VA 22555

Life & Liberty Publishing books are available at special discounts for bulk purchases by corporations, institutions and other organizations. For more information, please contact us at P.O. Box 638, Cheltenham, Maryland 20623, United States, or call toll free 866-656-7583.

Visit us on the web at libertylifeline.us

TABLE OF CONTENTS

Restoring American Freedom

We take as a given that the goal of the New World Order (NWO) oligarchy is to institute a two class society throughout the world consisting of a small and wealthy upper class, a large and poor lower class, and *no* middle class, a la Orwell's "1984." The middle class must today fight to preserve its existence. It is apparent that the American people have finally awakened to the peril closing in on them, and are taking steps to elect new legislators who will take that peril seriously.

I am herein offering up a sort of handbook to guide that new Congress to the core issues and to the legislative solutions which I believe must be implemented in order to save our country and its system of freedom for all. If this effort is successful, we may yet again set an example to people the world over who are hungering for such freedom.

In this effort, that magnificent creation called the Constitution of the United States will be my guide, along with some knowledge of about 225 years of our country's historical efforts to make our unique system work successfully, which I define as preserving the rights of our citizens to life, liberty, and the pursuit of happiness.

I have previously written four books covering 1) the identity of our major problems, 2) the legislative actions required to solve them, 3) the fact that the problems were deliberately created, 4) the identity and methods of the malefactors, and 5) the need for new legislators willing and able to enact the needed legislation. The present volume brings together the materials written in these four books, plus a few brand new thoughts, to summarize for those new legislators the legislative actions that I believe must be taken if we wish to restore our national well-being.

The material is divided into four categories: honesty issues, financial issues, non-financial domestic issues, and foreign issues, brief summaries of each of which follow.

Honesty Issues

In our present governmental system the oligarchy rules by

(1) Owning (or otherwise controlling) the major media,

(2) Buying candidates and fraudulent voting systems, and

(3) Controlling the legislative actions of their purchased legislators, thereby enhancing their own power and wealth and their consequent ability to maintain items 1 and 2.

This is a system that will assure that we have continuous war/peace cycles, an unchallenged financial system that enriches the oligarchs at the expense of our middle class via manufactured booms and busts, and a national debt that will forever increase to the point of the collapse of our economy and possible civil war, from which we will be "saved" by a Big Brother dictatorship, a la Napoleon.

We will describe in the first three chapters of this book how this cycle of dishonesty and corruption can be broken, requiring only an initial Congress having a sufficient number of Honest Constitutionalists (HC's) to emplace the first needed legislation. Chapter 1 describes how the monopoly power of the major media may be broken by the growing strength of an opposing Congress. Chapter 2 discusses how candidate selection and voting can then be made honest and kept in the hands of the electorate. Chapter 3 proposes a way of assuring that an elected candidate is truly an HC when he/she takes the oath of office before each new biennial congressional session. This system will keep the public fully and truthfully informed, will enable the public to elect the candidates it wants, and will assure that such candidates are true HCs.

Financial Issues

Four major items in this category need replacement or repair:

(1) Our monetary system, which has produced a huge unpayable national debt.

(2) Our intrusive income tax system, recommended by Karl Marx.

(3) Our fiscal system, which tolerates the spending which leads to our huge debts.

(4) Our tariff system, which has burdened us with a huge negative balance of trade and massive unemployment.

The Federal Reserve System will be replaced by the constitutional monetary system described in Chapter 4. The income tax and the IRS will be abolished and replaced by the tax on consumption described in Chapter 5, since economic growth and jobs are to be had by aiding the production process rather than discouraging it by taxation. Our fiscal system will be modified to preclude adding to the national debt, and to place a cap on the total tax load, as described in Chapter 6. Our tariff system, perhaps the main cause of our job losses, will be modified to be completely controlled by Congress, as described in Chapter 7.

Non-Financial Domestic Issues

There are four issues in this category, which will be addressed in this book:

(1) Reinstate the 10th Amendment,
(2) Apply the constitutional checks and balances,
(3) Destroy the illegal drug trade, and
(4) Fix the immigration system.

There exists a vast array of programs (retirement, medical and deposit insurance, loans and loan guarantees, welfare, education, etc.) which are in violation of the 10th Amendment, as they are not among the enumerated powers of Congress. They will be abolished or returned to the several states to manage, as described in Chapter 8.

The Constitution provides punishments which one branch of the government can impose upon another branch in the event of unconstitutional activity, such as making law by executive order or judicial decree, or failing to uphold the Constitution or any of the many laws promulgated under the same. The Congress should vigorously utilize these punishments (e.g., impeachment) to enforce the spread of constitutionalism into the executive and judicial branches, once the congressional branch has similarly restored itself via its Honest Constitutionalists. See Chapter 9.

Illegal drugs, being the largest source of off-the-books accumulations of ill-gotten gains by financial criminals, must be suppressed if a stable monetary system is ever to be successfully created and maintained. As discussed in Chapter 10, plenty of laws are already on the books to force the criminals in and out of government to be charged, tried, and jailed, most particularly those enabling the moving of drug money. If broken laws are not being enforced, those at fault should be impeached (per Chapter 9).

Illegal immigration has the potential of destroying the cohesion and the future well-being of the American people. Chapter 11 discusses how existing laws should be enforced (per Chapter 9) and added to.

Foreign Issues

There are three issues to be discussed in this category:
- (1) Avoid foreign entanglements,
- (2) Quit oligarchy's institutions, and
- (3) Create a World Freedom Institute.

Our present policies have gotten us into calamitous wars, huge debt, and the progressive loss of our personal freedoms. Under the secret direction of the oligarchy, the U.S. has been chosen to provide the muscle to bring about world changes that advance the oligarchy's program, including "regime changes," the support of foreign wars, the waging of U.S. wars for goals unrelated to our best interests, etc.

Chapter 12 sets a primary foreign policy goal: to stay out of the internal affairs of other countries and their international disputes, while at the same time maintaining sufficient economic and military strength to protect our own country from external attack.

Chapter 13 acknowledges that we ourselves are under attack by the oligarchy, and as soon as the Congress is back in our own hands we should quit their many agencies and commissions (e.g., the World Trade Organization) and work instead to resist their efforts to gain supremacy over us and the whole world.

Chapter 14 proposes that, after abdicating from the UN, we initiate the creation of a new organization of countries favoring individual freedom for its citizens, perhaps to be called The World Freedom Institute. The purposes and mechanics of such an organization are outlined.

Alan B. Jones
November 2010

Chapter 1

Give Public the Truth

The media system envisioned by Franklin, Jefferson, and others of our founders was supposed to keep a sharp eye out for corruption and for any excessive accumulation of political power anywhere within the government structure, in order to protect the public from any developing despotism. As history has shown, the media has failed to do so, and has instead become the purchased tool of the criminal oligarchs who would control us.

We believe that the elites of this world are close to their goal of destroying the American middle class, largely because they have successfully kept us in an ignorant stupor about even the existence of such an effort, simply by making sure that their effort never gets mentioned in any of the media which we read, see, or hear, the great bulk of which they own or otherwise control. We are instead fed a diet of praise for their New World Order agenda, plus "news" concerning men vs. women, liberals vs. conservatives, white vs. black, rich vs. poor, and any other x vs. y that they can think of *except* oligarchs vs. free citizens. So, how do we start reacquiring an honest, independent media?

We propose that Congress create a constitutionally and statutorially authorized program of generating and delivering news to the public, at congressional expense, on matters of concern to any group of members in Congress who believe that the private media's coverage of those matters has been inadequate.

We propose to start by having the Congress create and fund a Congressional News Service (CNS), the function of which would be to keep the public fully informed of the whole truth, as it is best known anywhere in the world. The CNS would manage the professional production of written and oral discussions of news events and concerns. They would be disseminated by contract to existing media and/or to new media created by or with the help of Congress, including print media, radio and TV networks, and Internet sites to enable computer display via printing and streaming video.

Real reporters would be hired and tasked to dig out the news, not just receive and report on departmental handouts. Separate staffs could be hired by any group in the Congress that desires such a staff, for the purpose of finding the facts on an issue, writing or recording their findings, and delivering them to both the old and the new media described above.

A number of separate reporting staffs would likely emerge, including one each for the two major parties. Other subgroups having reporting staffs might be Blue-dog Democrats, Progressives, the Black Caucus, and Honest Constitutionalists. Members of the subgroups would also be members of one or the other of the major party groups, so that such members would have a voice on issues both of their party and of their specialty.

A group or subgroup will be duly authorized and provided with the facilities described above, provided that a certain minimum number of congresspersons, say five, request such an authorization. Rescission of the authorization for any group or subgroup would require the unanimous vote of the members of the particular group or subgroup.

For historical archiving purposes, House and Senate rules should be written to provide for the materials generated by a group or subgroup to be considered duly approved by the Congress for inclusion in an adjunctive volume of the Congressional Record required by Article I, Section 5 of the Constitution. The rules should permit this record keeping and submission to the media even when the Congress is not in session. (Perhaps a congressional committee overseeing the operations of the Congressional News Service could stay in continuous session, even during congressional recesses.) The external media would therefore be in the legal position of simply reporting on materials submitted by Congress for ultimate printing in the Congressional Record.

To help ensure the honesty of the reports presented to the public, staffs tasked with generating and disseminating these news items would be required to take the same Truth Test as federal legislators, as described in Chapter 3.

We believe that the public will learn to love this service, and will shortly become aware of what they have been missing. At that point, private companies may perceive the desire of both the Congress and the public for real news, and may set about to acquire staff and facilities to serve that need, as Thomas Jefferson said was required. If the existing major media tries to block that newly rising competition, anti-trust action should be brought against the obvious cartel presently controlling news delivery in the United States. If governmental entities participate in the blockage, or oppose the anti-trust action, see Chapter 9 concerning impeachment.

If the issue does in fact become a major one discussed in the existing media, the public can be expected to join in the fray and support local news outlets who wish to display news not pre-approved by the oligarchy. The grass-roots attack and the national legal attack would be mutually supportive, and should be fought as publicly as possible. When the public begins to understand that they have been lied to for years, the battle will be essentially won, a result which many of us have been longing to see for many years.

Chapter 2

Ensure Election Honesty

In this chapter, we will take on five election honesty issues: 1) Electoral College, 2) electoral procedure, 3) campaign financing, 4) vote casting, and 5) vote counting.

1. Electoral College

We propose that the Electoral College provisions in the U.S. Constitution be repealed and that the election of President and VP be performed by the direct votes of the people in primary and general elections, in the same way as will be done for federal senators and representatives.

The Electoral College was designed for the days when contact between candidates and the electorate was difficult, expensive, and time consuming. That system of selecting electors who got together and held elections of the actual candidates solved the problem back then. Today, however, we have replaced buggy whips with airplanes, allowing the old system to be replaced by a modern, transparent one in which the whole electorate is involved with the outcome.

A number of anomalous and corrupt practices will disappear: No more electoral outcomes in which candidate X wins even though candidate Y received more votes. No more letting state politicians decide whether a state's electors will be "Winner take all" or will be split in proportion to voters' choices. No more caucuses in which the bulk of the voters are excluded by design or circumstances. No more overwhelming a smallish caucus by campaign managers with lots of money to spend on getting what they want. The public will be well served by finally ridding ourselves of the Electoral College system.

2. Electoral Procedure

We propose the following electoral procedure for the President and his VP (a joint candidacy) and the federal Senate and House members. Four possible elections will be scheduled, having uniform dates in all the states.

The first primary election, perhaps in April of an election year, will be an election to select, for each party wishing to participate in the election, a candidate to run for that party in the ultimate general election. If one individual receives a majority of the party's votes, that individual will be the party's candidate in the general election. If no individual receives a majority of the party's votes, a runoff election, perhaps in June, will be held between the party candidates receiving the most and the second most of the party's votes. The winner of that election will be the party's candidate in the general election.

The first general election, perhaps in September, will be an election to select the winners to take office. Any candidate receiving a majority of the cast votes is declared the winner. If no candidate receives a voting majority for a given office, the top two vote-getters will face each other in a runoff election, perhaps in November, to determine the final winner.

This system will make obsolete the presidential nominating conventions for each party, including the backroom deals that go with them, to select candidates for President and VP. Our new system, in accord with the founders' effort to create a government *by* the people, gives the public at large a major role in the selection of candidates for those offices.

Note also that this system will prevent third party tilting of presidential election results, like Teddy Roosevelt's 1912 Bull Moose effort which drained Republican votes from William Howard Taft, and elected Woodrow Wilson by a plurality of the votes. It is likely that merely providing for runoff elections will convince minor candidates not to waste their resources in mounting third-party efforts.

The individual states would be expected to use these same four election dates to hold their elections for state and local offices. Changes in state law may be needed to accomplish the needed schedule coordination and runoff election requirements. If that proves unworkable, a constitutional amendment should be introduced defining these changes.

3. Campaign Financing

In the area of campaign financing, two goals will be sought. First, if we are ever to create a government of and by the people rather than of and by the oligarchs, we must increase the representation in our legislatures of persons of moderate means, i.e., persons among the 90 percent of the population who can't presently compete. Second, we must prevent the "purchase" of candidates by donations from accumulated personal or organizational wealth, be it corporate, union, foundation, or other. Both of these goals will be furthered by the following reform.

In primary and general elections for federal office, including runoff elections, federal taxpayer dollars will be paid into a candidate's campaign account, which he will be required to open and maintain, to pay for an "adequate" campaign defined by statute, and covering the cost of a basic campaign infrastructure. The money provided should be in rough proportion to the size of the electorate for the particular office. A candidate or his supporters desiring to spend more than the "adequate" amount without the agreement of his opponent(s) to spend an equal excess amount could do so only if he agrees to fund and does promptly fund each of his opponents by an equal excess amount.

All campaign funds must be paid into and spent out of the candidate's campaign account. Donated services, like free TV time or other media exposure, having a free-market value greater than a defined statutory minimum, must appear as a credit in the campaign account when donated, and a debit when spent. The campaign account shall remain open on a read-only basis by governmental fair-election monitors, so that illegal spending can be easily detected. Stiff penalties shall be provided in law for violations.

States are invited to enact similar law governing their own state and local elections.

4. Vote Casting
Concerning vote casting, our goal is to permit only non-repetitive voting by legally registered voters. A federal statute should be enacted requiring that a person wishing to vote in federal elections must undergo a thorough local registration process. Proof of citizenship should be no less stringent than that required when applying for a U.S. passport, including birth certificate, citizenship papers if any, etc. To this end, an applicant for registration will be required to supply to the local voting registrar (or other voting official) his/her signature, full name, sex, birth date, place of birth, address of residence, birth certificate or equivalent, social security number (SSN), driver license number (DLN), and naturalization certificate number (NCN)

if a naturalized citizen. A full-face photo will be taken. If the applicant has moved from anywhere else in the U.S. where he had registered to vote, he must also supply his previous address and contact information for the previous registrar.

The current registrar will examine the proffered data by comparing it to state driver license files and federal social security and naturalization files, checking first that the supplied SSN, DLN, and NCN were issued to, and only to, the applicant, and then checking that the applicant has not had issued to him any other SSN, DLN, or NCN. The registrar will also verify whether or not the applicant physically lives at the address he claims, and that he is not identified as a felon in state records.

When the registrar is satisfied that the application data is valid and acceptable for approving the application, a registration certificate will be issued to the applicant, along with a (plastic) Voter Registration Card (VRC) which must be presented to precinct workers in his assigned precinct whenever he appears to vote on an election day. The VRC will contain the applicant's picture, signature, name, address, birth date, Voter Registration Number, and registrar contact information. The Voter Registration Number will identify the voter's state, county, precinct, and a numeric identity number within the precinct. If the applicant had previously been registered elsewhere in or outside the precinct, the registrar will notify the previous registrar of the new registration, whereupon the applicant's name will be removed from the old registration list.

The registrar shall be responsible for maintaining the currency of the registration list. He shall check it against death records, changes in property ownership, property tax records, etc. State law should be created calling for periodic state audits to be performed and publicly reported to determine whether maintenance of registration records is being performed in accordance with state and federal statutes.

On or just prior to election day, the registrar shall deliver the registration lists to the voting precincts. The precinct workers shall be required to check that an incoming voter is on the list, that the voter presents his Voter Registration Card and signs the registration list, that the data on the voter's VRC matches the registration list data, and that the voter's face and signature match the face and signature on the VRC. If everything matches satisfactorily, the voter is handed a ballot and directed to proceed with voting.

If, after registering, a voter is given and accepts the option to cast his vote by mail, he will be so permitted, and his option will be entered in the registration lists. Several weeks before the election, he will be sent a ballot identical to those given to voters in his normal precinct voting place. The envelope in which this absentee ballot will be returned to the county registrar will not show the voter's signature, birth date, or Voter Registration Number (VRN), but will have places for the voter to record those items on a portion of the envelope which cannot be seen when the envelope is sealed.

Upon receiving the envelope, the registrar will verify that the signature, birth date, and VRN written by the voter match the registration records. If they do, he will forward the marked ballot to the precinct on the election day, where the voting list will be marked to indicate that the voter had exercised his option to vote by mail. His ballot will then be placed in the ballot box with the other cast precinct ballots.

If the voter decides to deliver his marked absentee ballot to the precinct on election day rather than return it to the registrar, he may do so, and upon proper identification the voting list will be so annotated, and his ballot accepted.

5. Vote Counting

Concerning vote counting, we shall discuss the issues of ballot media, ballot number, computer source codes and functions, precinct counting, posting, and transmitting to the county, county summing, posting, and transmitting to the state, state summing, posting, and transmitting of unofficial results to the Federal Election Commissioner, interested party checking and resolution, and certifying the official results.

Our reform shall require that, in federal elections, voters shall record their votes on a medium which can be physically saved and visually interpreted, enabling later recounts by computer or by hand (without computers) if necessary. It shall be required that the ballots be safely retained by a County Voting Commissioner (hereinafter CVC) or other designated official to enable such a recount or for other checking purposes.

Each ballot in a precinct, including absentee ballots, will have a ballot number, known only to and retainable by the voter. That ballot number will appear on the ballot stub which the voter will detach and keep, and will also appear on the first page of the ballot where it will be read by the vote-tabulating computer and recorded along with the voter's choices.

The source language files of the computer codes installed in the precinct voting tabulators shall be made publicly available at least six months before the election, enabling others to copy and study the codes prior to the election as they may wish. The precinct computers shall be capable of reading a stack of voter ballots, computing totals for each ballot item, printing output data, and writing output data onto an external storage medium for physical transport elsewhere and for archival storage. The computer need not and shall not be connectable to any external computer or computer network.

On election day, the CVC shall assure that all absentee ballots are bundled and delivered to the correct precincts before the polls open, and that the official precinct computer equipment will be available and manned in each precinct prior to the close of voting. After the polls close, the physical ballots, including the absentee ballots received from the CVC, will be read into and counted by the precinct's computer. A summary edit will be printed, including the number of ballots processed and the voting totals for each item or candidate appearing on the ballot.

Also printed shall be the ballot number and voting choices made on each individual ballot, ordered by ascending ballot numbers. The summary edit and the individual ballot data will be posted in the precinct voting area. Both of these output files will also be written to the computer's external storage medium for physical delivery to the county and to the local media for public dissemination. These provisions will not only let a voter check that his votes were recorded as he wished, but will also discourage any downstream manipulation of the ballots during transmittals or later handling.

The vote totals will then be transmitted to the county along with the physical ballots and the annotated voter lists. In addition, if the number of ballots handed to voters plus the number of absentee ballots received from the CVC does not equal the number of ballots recorded on the computer printout, the precinct workers will try to find the cause of the discrepancy, but will in any event include a description of the discrepancy in their report to the CVC.

The county election officials will sum the results from all its precincts, and send those sums, along with the precinct inputs, back to the individual precincts and ask them to verify that the precinct inputs were correctly received and utilized. If correct, that verification is sent and recorded, and the precinct workers are done.

Only after all of the precinct inputs are verified may the county officials send their totals to the local media of record for public printing, and the totals for the state and federal races to the State Election Commissioner. That person will go through the same process of summing the county data, obtaining a recorded verification from every county of its inputs, and then releasing the state totals to the media for public dissemination. The public release of presidential election results must be delayed, however, until the polls are closed on the West Coast.

If a presidential election was on the ballot, the State Election Commissioner will send the federal election results to the Federal Election Commissioner. He will receive such data from all the states, and utilize the same process of summing across all the states, obtaining verification from each state, and then releasing the federal total to the media. This first federal result will be labeled "preliminary" if final resolution and certification is yet coming from any state, county, or precinct, although if a candidate is winning by a large margin, that result is likely to remain unchanged.

The final major addition related to vote counting we have called "interested party checking and resolution." It was noted above that precinct computer source codes were to be made available to the public to examine as they may wish. Computer techies can easily use these files to help them write functionally equivalent software in their own computers. The County Voting Commissioners should encourage the building of such computer systems, which would provide an independent check of the honesty and accuracy of the official precinct vote tabulating computers.

Sponsors of this checking function would likely be the Republican Party, the Democrat Party, any other party, or even non-party entities like a Truth in Politics organization. We will call such sponsors Interested Parties (IP's). An IP would also be required to make the source language of its software publicly available, so that others could read, understand, and compile and use it on their own computers.

All such IP computers must have the capability of reading a set of ballots, calculating vote totals, and building output files which can be visually displayed and/or printed. It must also be capable of reading the voting data written by the precinct's computer onto its external storage medium. Finally, it must contain comparison software to compare the precinct voting data to the data regenerated by the IP computer, and, if mismatches between these two sets of data are found, to display and/or print the details of such mismatches.

Before the election, the CVC will, upon the request of an IP, provide a number of marked up test ballots which will be loaded into the CVC's official computer and also into the IP's computer. If the output printouts of the two systems are functionally identical, and if the IP's comparison software works satisfactorily, the CVC will designate that IP as one of the verifiers of the precinct ballots received by the county.

When the CVC first receives the precinct's report and its output data, he will try to resolve any discrepancies reported by the precinct, and accordingly modify the vote counts he previously sent to the state. Likewise, he may further modify the vote counts in accordance with discrepancies discovered by the IP comparison which he was able to resolve. His final summary report to the state shall include the adjusted county vote count and the number of remaining unresolved anomalies.

The State Election Commissioner, having received such data from all the counties, shall send the modified results to the Federal Election Commissioner, and will announce the certified state winners if the number of unresolved anomalies is small enough to have no effect on the result of any state election. Otherwise, further recount efforts by county and state election officers may be initiated.

Chapter 3

Truth-Test Winning Candidates

In the section of our Introduction dealing with Honesty Issues, we discussed the need to get a few Honest Constitutionalists (HC's) into the Congress to initiate the next steps: creating a media which will get honest information about public affairs to the public, creating an honest election system, and creating a formal system for determining with high accuracy whether a federal candidate is or is not an HC. We believe that the 2010 election has in fact gotten a few HC's into Congress, and they can help mightily in creating that formal system.

The big problem is that lying as a deliberate strategy frequently pays, with the public being the chief loser, as is thoroughly discussed from an historical viewpoint in References 3 and 4. Thus, in our present legislative environment, particularly in Washington, DC, legislators are sworn in with a promise to "protect and defend the Constitution of the United States," but what most of them really intend to protect and defend are their own emoluments, perquisites, and chances of reelection. Far too commonly the operative mechanism to that end, which is usually implied or understood but rarely verbalized, is "Do as we want and we'll help you in your next election. If you don't, we'll run and support someone who will."

Our republic cannot survive with legislative majorities corrupted in this fashion by the fattest of the world's fat cats, and we can all see our ship of state filling with water from the institutional rot and nearing the onset of sinking. We propose drastic action to plug the leaks, pump out the water, and set sail on a voyage toward freedom for all. The action we propose is to require incoming lawmakers to submit to a brief lie detector test as a qualification for being seated in the Congress. The contents of the test will be defined in law, and will be made well known to the public. We will hereinafter call it the Truth Test. It will contain the following three relevant questions sandwiched among a few irrelevant (but necessary) control questions:

TRUTH-TEST WINNING CANDIDATES

1. Have you read and thought about the questions you are about to be asked?

2. Do you have a good understanding of the provisions and purposes of the U.S. Constitution?

3. Is your desire to preserve the freedoms of our citizens under the Constitution greater than your desire to preserve or advance your own economic or political future?

4. Please answer no to this question. Have you ever driven above the posted speed limit?

5. Do you hold an allegiance to the United States, its Constitution, and its citizens above your allegiance or subservience to any person, organization, ideology, country, or other entity having goals in conflict with the U.S., its Constitution, or its citizens?

6. Please answer no to this question. Do you sometimes drink water?

Ref. 3, pp. 326-329, puts the situation this way:

"If a government can see fit to administer [lie detector] examinations to those it hires to develop the country's weapons of war, how much greater should be the incentive to examine those whose job it will be to write the laws defining the policies by which the country will operate?

"…Observe what it is that we have done. We have rejected the notion that all we can do is mount a rear-guard action, seeking, as we retreat, to occasionally win a skirmish or two (like beating back fast-track). On the contrary, we have decided, like the army general or the football coach, that without an offense, we will surely lose in the long run, no matter how strong our defense might be. We must, therefore, develop and put in the field a vigorous, credible, viable offense aimed at *defeating* our opponents. If we fail to do so, we are headed for a worldwide Dark Age out of which the world's humanity may *never* emerge, so powerful and astute are our opponents. Our efforts go beyond simply trying to educate the public about each of the new outrages which our wannabe masters perpetrate. We seek instead to stop them, emasculate them, and take back the control of our country."

Our corrupt legislators may be expert and successful liars when addressing other human beings, but they will find it virtually impossible to fool our modern Voice Stress Analysis technology (extensively described in

Ref. 4), which does not suffer from human emotional weaknesses. All that is required is for the subject to speak clear yes or no answers into a digital voice recorder in response to the few Truth Test questions listed above. The voice record will be sent to one or more professional Voice Stress Analysis examiners. A written verdict will shortly be returned to the subject for him to do with as Congress may require by law, but otherwise as he himself may wish. If he passes the test, he will also receive a Truth in Politics Certificate so attesting.

We'll describe first how the system will work when fully operational, and then deal with a congressional strategy for getting to that point.

1.   The tests will be required of all federal legislative candidates, either incumbent or challenger, as an integral element of every biennial election.

2.   A month or so before the prescribed date for primary elections, federal legislative and presidential candidates will be offered, but will not be required, to take the Truth Test, enabling candidates to utilize the test results in their election campaigns if they so desire. Minor party candidates can decline to be tested with little consequence.

3.   Taking the test will also be a required qualification for congressional seating (Art. I, Sect. 5). Being aware of this requirement, a candidate would do well to take the test early (e.g., before the primary election), as the public would doubtless expect. That testing will thereby be completed well before the active days of starting up a new congressional session.

4.   It is expected that those candidates who pass the Truth Test will be quick to make those results public, and to proudly display their Truth in Politics Certificates.

5.   The formal swearing in ceremonies of the House and Senate will not be altered by anything in this new system.

6.   In the first year with a sufficient HC presence, Congress will create an entity, e.g., the Congressional Truth Commission (CTC), and appoint a number of interim Members, half public and half congressional. Those interim Members shall elect one

of their group to be the interim Chairman. The CTC will be authorized to keep the test records (who, when, where, test giver, etc.) and to appoint interim Managers in each state. These State Managers will seek out motivated citizen voters to take on the task of administering the Truth Test to federal legislative candidates. The mailing lists of HC supporters in the 2010 election may aid in locating such motivated Test Givers. Prior to their interim appointments as CTC Chairman and Members, State Managers, and Test Givers, such persons must themselves take and pass the Truth Test.

7. During biennial non-election years, the CTC members and officers will be elected or reelected from the bottom up. That is, the state Test Givers will elect or reelect, from among the members of their own groups, the State Managers. The State Managers will in turn elect or reelect the CTC Members, the candidates for which shall be taken from incumbents, from State Managers, and from congressional nominees. Finally, the CTC Members will elect or reelect the CTC Chairman. By this process, all the first-year interim top-down appointments will be superseded by the described bottom-up electoral procedure, a process that will be repeated every two years, mirroring the biennial elections to the House of Representatives.

8. All personnel in the CTC and in the state testing organizations must also periodically take and pass the Truth Test, at a periodicity specified by the CTC Members. The records of such testing will be sent to and archived by the CTC. All that archived data shall be freely available to the State Managers.

9. The testing path for any given candidate is as follows:

   a. A testing offer is tendered to the candidate.

   b. ·The candidate accepts or declines.

   c. Upon acceptance, a Test Giver is assigned and administers the test. The resulting voice file contains a test number but no identification of the candidate.

d. The voice file is transmitted via an email attachment to the State Manager, who transmits it in turn to one of several Examination Managers.

e. The Examination Manager assigns the analysis to two independent examiners.

f. The two examiners examine the voice file, and transmit back to the Examination Manager their diagnoses of deception or no deception indicated on each of the relevant questions.

g. The Examination Manager certifies the diagnosis as Fail if both examiners diagnose "Deception Indicated" on the same relevant question, otherwise Pass. He returns his report to the State Manager.

h. The State Manager returns a written Pass/Fail report to the candidate, along with a Truth in Politics Certificate if the candidate passed the test.

i. The Examination Manager and his two examiners will not know the identity of the candidate, and the candidate will not know the identity of the examiners.

10. The testing of CTC personnel runs a similar path, except that the result will be Fail if *either* examiner finds Deception Indicated on any relevant question.

11. Once this testing system has produced a much higher proportion of Honest Constitutionalists in the Congress than at present, attention might be given by that Congress to the application of this system throughout the Executive and Judicial Branches. One obvious move in that direction would be to require all executive branch appointees that are subject to Senate confirmation, including Cabinet officers and Supreme Court justices, to take and pass the Truth Test as a condition of their confirmation.

How can we proceed from the present (early 2011) state of affairs to the honest system described above? None, or very little, of Chapters 4 through 14 can be accomplished without a much stronger HC presence in the Congress. Getting that added strength may be accomplished with the help of the media, election, and Truth Testing reforms described in Chapters 1-3. The first priority, therefore, is for the small group of HC's in the present Congress to focus and work diligently on advancing the reforms discussed in chapters 1-3.

To get started, existing HC legislators should identify themselves to each other and form a joint HC Caucus. Discuss this plan in the caucus. Those HCs willing to lead the charge should arrange to take the Truth Test ASAP, in order to test the testing system, and to set a few examples for other more wary Constitutionalists. After this beginning, it should be required of other HC's desiring to join the coalition that they read this book, take the Truth Test, pass it, prominently display their Truth in Politics Certificates, and then relate their actions to the general congressional membership.

Starting with the media issue described in Chapter 1, define in the HC Caucus which congressional groups and subgroups may wish to participate in a Congressional News Service (CNS). With their help and backing, define and introduce the legislation concerning the creation and operation of the CNS and the new media that may have to be created. A constitutional amendment may be needed, to wit: Add to Art. I Section 8 the clause "To provide for the delivery to the public of true information on public and governmental affairs." Hire the needed reporting staffs, all having passed the Truth Test, and provide for the archival storage of the generated and disseminated news. Try to get that media system into operation by early 2012, so as to be available during the election campaigns in that year.

In the HC Caucus, define the legislation proposed in Chapter 2 concerning honest elections, and introduce it, including:

(1) A Constitutional Amendment abolishing the Electoral College, and providing for voting by the people for joint President-Vice President candidacies.

(2) A Constitutional Amendment (if necessary) to require runoff elections between the top two vote-getters in primary or general elections for federal office in which no candidate received a majority of the cast votes; and to require all such primary, general, and runoff elections to be held on the same dates in every State.

(3) Legislation (or a Constitutional Amendment if deemed

necessary) providing for public payment to federal candidates for a legislatively defined "adequate" campaign. Candidates may receive and spend money and services in excess of those limits only if they simultaneously contribute to each of their opponents the same amount of excess funds, including the value of any excess services.

(4) Legislation requiring that a voter in a federal election present, when appearing to vote in a local precinct, his (federally funded) Voter Registration Card containing a photo ID, signature, and other identification data, issued by the local voting registrar upon the voter's presentation and the registrar's verification of his proof of citizenship and of all other data required by his state. The proof of citizenship shall be no less stringent than that required when applying for a passport.

(5) Legislation requiring that in federal elections voters shall record their votes on a medium which can be physically saved and visually interpreted, enabling manual recounts if necessary; that the initial reading and totalizing and posting of individual ballot and precinct total results, and the transmission of said results to local media, shall be done in the precincts by the precinct workers; that if computers are used to read and totalize the ballots, the source language of the computer software shall be made public by at least six months before the election; and that verification by independently programmed backup computers shall be encouraged and utilized if any independent party so desires and is so authorized by the local county voting commissioner or equivalent.

Perhaps a good portion of those election reform issues may be in place in time for the 2012 elections.

The HC Caucus should start the process of creating the Congressional Truth Commission (CTC), as described in this Chapter 3. HC Caucus members should take the Truth Test, get their Truth in Politics Certificates, and advertise these activities among the general congressional membership and in the present media. Those HC Caucus members who would like to participate in the CTC and who have passed the Truth Test should forthwith create the interim CTC and elect an interim Chairman and other (tested) staff as deemed necessary. The interim CTC may then begin the process of finding and appointing interim State Managers, and tasking them to find motivated Test Givers to administer the Truth Test to federal candidates. (For merging with the corresponding grass roots effort, see www.atipa.org.)

Discuss and resolve funding policies, probably involving fees from the public Test Givers, plus some level of congressional support. Formulate and introduce legislation, or perhaps just congressional rules, formalizing these actions, including rules making submission to Truth Testing a qualification for seating an incoming legislator (Article I, Section 5), in order to assure permanent government involvement in and endorsement of this system.

Chapter 4

Fix Monetary System

1. All demand and time deposit accounts in U.S. banks must hereafter be continually backed by reserves of real cash or cash equivalent (e.g., U.S. bonds) to cover 100% of the ongoing payable liabilities of those accounts. Further, the banks may not make loans from demand deposit reserves. No more bank runs!

2. A U.S. bank may lend at interest funds in its "loan reserve," which may include the bank's surplus, its time deposits, and government bonds which it has purchased (which will be replaced by cash upon their sale or ultimate redemption). The bank may not make any loan (e.g., a mortgage) if its loan reserve is less than the proposed loan. The bank must also never permit its loan reserve to go negative, i.e., it must look ahead to anticipate reductions in its loan reserve as scheduled withdrawals are made from its time deposits. Interbank rediscounting will remain useful. By these means, a 100% reserve system is maintained, borrowers can only borrow what someone else has saved, and no new currency is lent into existence! There will no longer be uncontrolled multiplicative creation, lending, depositing, recreation, relending, redepositing, etc., via which the banks are presently controlling the volume of our circulating currency as they may see fit (or find financially advantageous). To assure that this change reaches into the future, the "To coin Money" paragraph of Article I, Section 8 of the Constitution should be amended to read: "The Congress shall have the Power... To exercise the exclusive Rights to coin U.S. Money of Gold and Silver, to issue legal tender Bills redeemable in said Money, to regulate the Value thereof, and of foreign Coin, and to fix the Standard of Weights and Measures."

3. Selling a mortgage (or other asset) to a third party buyer to raise money to make further loans will be permitted only if the bank

agrees to retain the financial responsibility for servicing such a mortgage, including the transmission of its income to the buyer, the adjustment of its terms, and the absorption of any ultimate loss upon its default. This process may be undertaken on a large scale, selling bundled and honestly valued assets created under the fractional reserve system which cannot be retained under the 100% reserve system. The money for such sales exists in the huge quantity of U.S. bonds held by Americans, Europeans, Asians (especially Chinese), and others who may welcome the increased income from such assets over what is presently available in interest on the U.S. bonds. The ESA (item 8 below) may be tasked to review and approve the valuation of such bundled assets, with the full participation of buyers and their representatives.

4. Congress will acquire all of the twelve Federal Reserve Banks by purchasing at par value all the stock of those banks, or by any other available means. Those banks will henceforth be owned, staffed, and managed (or disposed of) by the U. S. Treasury, in accordance with the wishes of the U.S. Congress, based upon its constitutional mandate to "coin money and regulate the value thereof." Except for the bank stock, the entirety of the Fed's assets and liabilities will be merged into the Treasury.

5. The Fed's asset of Treasury Gold Certificates (a "lien" on Treasury gold), its asset of U.S. bonds, and its liability of Treasury deposits will all be extinguished upon their return to the Treasury. This action will, in and of itself, produce a significant reduction in the national debt.

6. The Fed's surplus, its assets other than U.S. bonds (e.g., member bank cash reserves), and its liabilities of time and demand FRN deposits will be assumed by the U.S. Treasury. Loan assets may, if desired, be sold off to investors.

7. FRN accounts which are determined to be legally sourced and on the regular books of worldwide banks or other financial institutions will, upon the request of such an institution, henceforth be denominated in congressionally authorized gold-backed (per Art.

I, Section 8 of the Constitution), non-interest bearing notes herein called Treasury Gold Certificates (TGCs), which will become our replacement circulating currency. Similarly, legally sourced U.S. government bonds held by such institutions (e.g., China) will, prior to or upon their maturity, be paid off by issues of TGCs created for that purpose. Our national debt will, thereby, be paid off.

8. An Economic Stabilization Agency (ESA) will be created by, managed by, and be answerable to the Congress, per Article I, Section 8 of the Constitution. Its purposes will be (1) to permanently minimize unemployment (presently in double digits), (2) to maintain the constant long term purchasing power of the dollar (presently worth about 5% of its 1940 value), and (3) to otherwise promote a permanent high standard of living for the (long-suffering) American middle class (of, by, and for whom the U.S. Government was promulgated). The ESA's actions will be to recommend to the Congress policies and actions regarding regulation of the monetary system (i.e., expansion or contraction of the circulating medium of exchange) and of world trade (see Chapter 7). Stabilizing the value of the dollar will enable saving to be a rational act again, setting the stage for utilizing annuitization for retirement income and end-of-life medical expenses.

9. If the economy is tending toward deflation, the ESA will direct that the volume of the active medium of exchange ("money") be increased by tax reductions, and/or by the creation and time-deposit of new TGCs into our country's banks (where they will be available for lending), and/or by new TGCs being spent into circulation by increased government expenditures (e.g., for infrastructure improvement or payment of some portion of any remaining national debt). Long-term population growth will tend (slowly) to produce such deflation, and will require a proportional increase in the actively circulating medium of exchange.

10. If the economy is tending toward inflation, the ESA will direct that TGCs be withdrawn from circulation by means of increased taxation, lowering of the Treasury's TGC accounts in the country's banks, reduction of government expenditures, etc.

11. The ESA will continuously monitor the balance of trade with other countries, and recommend appropriate action by the Congress, as discussed in Chapter 7.

12. The ESA will determine, and from time to time may modify, the "price" of gold into which a TGC may be redeemed. Assume that the volume of the medium of exchange needed to support a "full employment economy" may be approximated by the total of circulating FRNs and demand deposits at some recent "normal" point in our economic history, say 2001. Divide that figure, say 1000 billion dollars, by the present stock of Treasury gold, say 0.25 billion ounces, yielding a gold "price" of 4000 dollars per ounce. If more gold then arrives at the Treasury, as it probably will at that price, to total say 0.4 billion ounces, the price would be reduced to 1000/0.4 = 2500 dollars per ounce. The new dollar, or TGC, would thus be defined as 1/2500 = 0.00040 ounces of gold, and the Treasury would hold 1000 billion dollars worth of gold, into which TGCs could be redeemed. Some limitation on foreign redemption might be needed until the bulk of the outstanding foreign-held bonds are gradually reduced by maturity, payoff, and reinvestment into long-term financial vehicles (e.g., time deposits in worldwide banks, including U.S. banks).

Chapter 5

Replace Income Tax

This chapter deals with the abomination which is the intrusive federal income tax, personal and corporate. It is to be abolished, along with the IRS and the whole tax preparation industry. The 16th Amendment authorizing the income tax will be repealed to prevent the tax from easily reappearing. A horde of bureaucrats and other tax preparers may then set about to find more productive employment.

The policy behind the tax structure that is herein proposed is to help build our economic well-being by encouraging investment in the production process by not taxing that process or the investment activities that finance it. We will therefore not tax income from savings (interest income) or business investment (dividends, capital gains) or business profits or personal income from participating in that process. We will tax instead the sale of the products and services which that production process creates.

Specifically, the federal income tax will be replaced by a uniform sales tax on all previously untaxed goods and services (excepting only food) purchased abroad or purchased domestically from state-licensed or regulated foreign or domestic businesses, for consumption by domestic not-for-profit entities (i.e., by non-business U.S. consumers). The tax will be collected by the several states and transmitted to the U.S. Treasury, one check per quarter per state. Such taxation can easily and rapidly be adjusted under the direction of the ESA (Chap. 4, item 8) in accordance with its needs (Chap. 4, items 9 and 10).

Note that the present system taxes heavily the higher incomes associated with production leaders, but only lightly (if at all) those in the lower income ranges. The new system does much the same. If you have a high income or great wealth, you will be taxed when and if you spend it on some desired good or service, including doctors, lawyers, housekeepers, accountants, yachts, new houses, world travel, etc.. If you have a small income and little wealth, you won't spend as much, so you won't pay as much taxes – none at all on food, one of the large budget items for a low-income family, percentagewise. However, all persons, rich or poor, will pay at least *something* in order for everyone to know that they have a stake in our American system and in the doings of our government.

A constitutional amendment may be required to authorize a federal sales tax, such a tax being in violation of Article I, Section 9 of the Constitution, as was the income tax.

A PRIMER FOR A CONSTITUTIONALIST CONGRESS | 25

Chapter 6

Fix Fiscal System

We shall focus in this chapter on two aspects of our federal fiscal system: how to enforce a balanced budget, and how to limit the total tax load on the public. If we can deal successfully with these two matters, we should be able, over a period of time, to replace our entire national debt with a substantial emergency reserve, while permanently maintaining the total tax load on our citizens to a specified tolerable level.

We take on first the matter of creating annual budget surpluses. Our proposal is simply this: instead of authorizing a specific dollar amount that each department of government may spend, Congress shall instead authorize only that each department may spend a specified percentage of whatever the total revenues for the next year are estimated to be (excepting the Treasury Department's expenditures for interest on any remaining debt). No "off-budget items" will be permitted to exist. The authorized percentages shall be constrained to always add up to 100.

If during the budgeting process a department's percentage is increased to accommodate a new expenditure, the percentages for all other departments shall be automatically reduced, so that the 100 percent total is mathematically maintained. During the course of the subsequent fiscal year, any additional spending authorized by the Congress for a given department shall be made only at the expense of reducing the authorized spending proportionally for all the other departments. As the fiscal year progresses, revenues shall be tracked against those that were expected, and quarterly adjustments will correspondingly be computed in each department's spending authorization for the year and delivered to those departments for implementation.

The budgets so created shall include an item for paying down the national debt and ultimately replacing it with a rainy day surplus. (We *must* stop asking unborn generations to pay for our current "needs"!) National debt reduction might comprise about three or four percent of the total budget. Debt coming due in excess of that amount will not be rolled over, but will be paid off with TGCs created for that purpose, as described in Chapter 4.

A specific budget allocation should also be made to accommodate any contingent expense that might reasonably be expected during the coming fiscal year. Such expenses may be uncertain, but they should nevertheless be estimated as accurately as possible, and those estimates included as an authorized percentage of the total budget.

If at the end of the fiscal year expenditures have proven to be less than revenues, the difference will be returned to the states in proportion to their actual annual payments. If, on the other hand, expenditures have exceeded government receipts, the states will be billed to make up the difference, also in proportion to each state's actual payment. This provision will *assure* that the federal budget remains in balance, and that a gradual reduction in the national debt will actually occur. It will also give state politicians a strong stake in the federal budget's remaining in balance. The state's federal senators and congressmen will feel similar motivations, as they will be reluctant to face reelection just after their state and its taxpayers have been billed to pay off its share of a federal deficit.

To ease the mechanics of this reform, the various departments of the government will define, at the beginning of the fiscal year's budgeting process, how their operations may be adjusted during the coming year to accommodate changes in budget authorizations by the Congress in response to changes in realized revenues, added or deleted budget items, etc. Each department should therefore prepare and submit to the Congress contingency plans for modified authorizations (up or down) as a part of its annual budget request. These plans should include such provisions as the addition, deletion, or deferral of budget items, the substitution of higher or lower cost alternatives, the increase or reduction of salaries or staffing levels, etc.

Congress, for its part, should be satisfied to review and approve a department's plans as to what measures it will take in order to stay within a variable budget during the course of a fiscal year. The department will have defined its priorities, as it perceives them, in the writing of its contingency plan. The Congress will perhaps modify, but will then approve that contingency plan, so that the Congress will also be aware of what will and will not be done within the department as the money available to it may change during the course of the fiscal year.

Congress should give this procedure a trial run, and if it works well should undertake to enforce it upon future Congresses. To this end, a constitutional amendment should be introduced requiring the Congress to create annual balanced budgets, and if any residual unbalance exists at the end of a fiscal year between revenues and expenditures, that unbalance shall be made up by remitting to or billing the states for the unbalance.

We'll examine next the issue of the total tax load on our citizenry. Back in the time period around 1960, just before the Vietnam War and LBJ's Great Society, our economy was still growing, and taxes were not so high as to be seriously affecting that growth. However, this time also defined the beginning of the long-term slowdown of our economic growth. We propose that 1960 be used to define our maximum taxation criterion. At that time, the total of federal, state, and local taxes were taking about 25 percent of our national income, while the federal tax alone was taking about 18 percent, which is $18/25 = 72\%$ of the total taxation. That ratio is likely to change from time to time, particularly as governmental functions are shifted between federal and state, e.g., by the changes defined in Chapter 8.

Our proposed reform is simply that, at the beginning of its deliberations on the next year's budget, the Congress should ask for and receive figures on the previous year's national domestic product (NDP) and the total of received state and local taxes. The federal budget limit for the new year will then be determined by computing 25 percent of that NDP, and then subtracting the state and local received taxes. The remainder is the top limit of what the federal government can budget for the new year.

Note that this procedure puts the state and local governments in the position of being able to first satisfy themselves, with the federal government having to conform thereto. This arrangement is deliberate, and is aimed at protecting the rights of the politically weaker and economically smaller units (the states), while forcing the more profligate organization (the federal) to limit itself to a budget that will limit our total tax load to 25 percent of the national product.

It is the federal legislature, of course, which is the primary target of our reform, and the reform as outlined, along with the balanced budget reform, will force the needed discipline upon the Congress. The system will provide incentives both on the part of federal legislators to hold down state expenditures, and also on the part of state legislators to hold down federal expenditures. Advices on doing so should fly back and forth, to the benefit of the nation's taxpayers

To mechanize this reform, Congress should develop and write into law formulae for unambiguously computing annual gross national product from statistics which are or can be made readily available. Once the federal sales tax becomes operative, the NDP might be taken as the sum of the annual sales of products and services subject to that new tax (plus sales of food) which the states, as collectors of the tax, should have immediately available. The states can also readily report on received state and local tax revenues for that year, completing the data needed to determine the maximum permitted federal tax load for the upcoming year.

Defining the tax load criterion as a percentage of GDP permits it to be expressed independently of the economic ups and downs that will occur. As such, the criterion can and should be permanently written into our legal system via a constitutional amendment, where it can act as a real bar to its being ignored by our government.

A word should be said about short-term financial "emergencies" which may call for rapid action When one of these arises, as no doubt it will, the government may deal with it via the following hierarchy of actions: 1) budget it in the next fiscal year; 2) include it in the current budget, but automatically reduce all other budget items as needed to leave the total unchanged; 3) if the other items cannot be sufficiently reduced, and if an emergency reserve has been maintained in the Treasury, increase the budget total to the statutory budget cap, and pay for the emergency out of a combination of the Treasury reserve and reduced expenditures previously budgeted. This action will require billing the states for the increase at the end of the fiscal year.

If money is needed in excess of the budget cap, it may be raised by the "emergency" means listed in items 4, 5, and 6 below. The expenditure of such funds, however, shall not be included in the calculation of the fiscal year deficit to be billed to the states. The emergency means are: 4) pay for the excess over the cap by withdrawing funds from the carefully accumulated emergency reserve referred to above; 5) if still more is needed, borrow by selling bonds (to American citizens and corporations only), creating or increasing the federal debt; 6) if national survival requires it, inflate the currency by issuing the additionally needed TGCs, as noted in Chapter 4 above, but with the intention of withdrawing them via taxation as quickly as possible.

Issuing such currency without adding any corresponding gold backing constitutes, of course, the classical act of inflation, and if the currency is not withdrawn, will cause rising prices, including an increase in the long-term gold redemption price. Devalued TGCs will be redeemable in a little less gold, and the stored value of all TGC-denominated savings diminished. The governmental issue of unbacked currency will be shown once more to amount to nothing more than a hidden tax forced on those holding fixed dollar-denominated assets.

Thus, it may be seen that our proposed budgeting system really will provide the flexibility needed to accommodate budget emergencies, provided that the Congress has had the foresight to budget for bailouts, to budget well below statutory budget caps, and to assure that adequate reserves of currency are maintained in the Treasury.

Chapter 7

Fix Tariff System

Protective tariffs are not new. They were put in place under Presidents James Monroe and John Quincy Adams. The predecessors of today's oligarchs pressured Congress, and the tariffs were rescinded in 1833. The Second Bank of the U.S. had been closed in 1832, leaving British banks in control of credit, which they promptly withdrew, causing the collapse of the economy in 1837. (Note that this collapse could not have occurred had the banking system defined in Chapter 4 been in place. Nor could it have in 2008.) The public in subsequent years threw out the anti-tariff "Free Traders" and elected the Whigs William Henry Harrison and several years later General Zachary Taylor, both of whom died abruptly and mysteriously, leaving weaker and more manipulable presidents in place.

Today, we will try again to replace our British "free trade" system, which was originally designed to suck wealth out of its colonies. The system is presently managed by the oligarchs' World Trade Organization. Our new system will be designed to maintain a zero balance of trade, enabling the regrowth of America's productive capacity, with good jobs for all who are capable and desirous of working.

A tariff imposed on an imported good or service is a tax, owed by an importer and paid to the U.S. government, equal to a specified percentage, say 5%, of the price of the item paid by the importer to the foreign exporter. If the importer is going to resell the item to a distributor or store for ultimate sale, he will ordinarily pass on the cost of the tariff to that distributor, who will pass it on to the final purchaser. Domestic producers of the same item will thereby be given a sales price advantage equal to the tariff percentage, which will tend to bring the production process back to the U.S.

Note that if a sales tax is in effect (see Chapter 5), it will be imposed on top of the tariff-enhanced purchase price. In addition, if the importer is himself the final non-business consumer of the foreign good or service, he will owe the government both the tariff and the sales tax.

How will our new system work? We will apply such a tariff only against the goods and services imported from countries with which we have a negative balance, such as China. For each such country, a country-specific tariff will be imposed which will be periodically adjusted to keep the balance of trade close to zero. The ESA (Chapter 4) will continuously monitor that balance of trade, and make its recommendations for change to the Congress, which is specifically empowered "to regulate commerce with foreign nations" (Art. I Section 8 of the Constitution). The tariff will be imposed on imports of all that country's goods and services (including both manufacturing services and individual labor) except those designated by the Congress as national security needs which cannot be produced domestically.

To define our present problem, if we buy very much more from a given country (e.g., China) than we sell to it, their accumulated dollars are much more than our accumulation of their currency, making it possible and expedient for China to pay for her purchases from us with her accumulated dollars rather than her own currency. If we simply require that that be done, then we will no long have any concern about the value of her currency, as we will never handle it. Our trade balance over a defined period of time is then simply dollars in minus dollars out. That is presently a monstrous negative value, but one which can quickly be reduced by the application of a tariff. No discharge of imbalances via movement of gold will be permitted, or will be needed, permitting our gold to serve its primary function of imparting domestic confidence in the permanence and utility of our monetary system.

Following the startup of our new monetary system, a new Bretton Woods conference should be held to define the adjusted exchange rates for the various national currencies around the world. An agreed upon basket of commodities available in any country could be used for that purpose, by means of which financial planning and interchanges around the world would be facilitated. If a country then persists in arbitrarily manipulating its currency for non-transparent purposes, other countries can choose to do business with them, if they wish, in terms of barter or just their own currency.

Maintaining a net zero balance of trade with the rest of the world will promote the twin goals of expanding jobs for our middle class while simultaneously protecting American sovereignty and the value of our dollar.

Chapter 8

Reinstate Tenth Amendment

The framers of the Constitution found that to get it ratified they needed to add a Bill of Rights, listing many of the important things that the new government could *not* do, like make laws abridging the freedom of speech. Then they added the 9th Amendment, saying there were lots of other freedoms that could have been listed, and then added perhaps the most important, the 10th Amendment, saying that the new government's rights were limited to just those that were enumerated in the Constitution.

Later politicians managed to slither around the 10th Amendment by loosely interpreting the last sentence of Article I Section 8, which gave Congress the power "To make all laws necessary" to execute all the other enumerated powers. Thus arose the conflict between the "strict constructionists" like Thomas Jefferson and those who, like Alexander Hamilton, felt that "necessary" should be interpreted as "needful, requisite, incidental, useful, or conducive to," in support of his view that a government should have a sovereign right to exercise any means required to attain the ends of the powers granted to it.

Hamilton's views prevailed over Jefferson's regarding the first national bank, and were borrowed and used again by Chief Justice John Marshall in justifying his 1819 Supreme Court decision upholding the constitutionality of the second Bank of the United States. We have lived to deplore the results of permitting the means to be justified by desirable ends, and are today inundated in evidence of the bad governmental outcomes which have resulted. This chapter will list some of these outcomes, all in violation of the strict constructionist view of the 10th Amendment.

We will address three categories of issues: (1) benefits to individuals, (2) federal largesse in the form of bailouts, insurance, loan guarantees, etc., and (3) miscellaneous.

Starting off with individual benefits, we note that there is nothing in the Constitution granting the federal government the authority to spend public money on benefits for individual citizens, excepting payments for education (GI bill) and medical services (VA hospitals) for military retirees as a form of payment for their military service. Benefit programs for individual citizens should all be returned to the states, including social security and other federal retirement programs, Medicare and other federal medical insurance programs, and a clutch of federal welfare programs.

In fact, the Congress might profitably beef up the Bill of Rights by adding another amendment specifically prohibiting the Congress from making any law respecting the health, education, welfare, feeding, housing, clothing, or fiscal support of its citizens. The states would then be responsible for defining their handling of these matters. Proposed actions to replace the major individual benefit programs follow.

INDIVIDUAL BENEFITS — SOCIAL SECURITY

Social Security is a Ponzi game, which its replacement will not be. FDR got it passed by convincing taxpayers that it was a social good for those working to build up their own retirement funds and to help support hard-pressed seniors. His method was not sustainable, however, as it degenerated into workers supporting retirees, not retirees accumulating their own retirement of real dollars that were theirs. FDR's Ponzi scheme is now running out, with not enough workers joining the ranks at the bottom to support the ever-increasing number of beneficiaries. Current workers have begun to doubt that their social security taxes will ever provide them *any* retirement income. Their worry is justified, since *no funds* were ever set aside to pay retirees, the social security taxes having all been "borrowed" and spent by the Congress on other government expenses. The Social Security Administration (SSA) was left with a pile of non-negotiable IOUs for its misappropriated funds, payable by the government only by extracting more taxes from the public. An insurance company pulling off the same caper would soon find its officers in the slammer.

The Social Security system will be replaced by a much better system which will take advantage of the stabilization of our currency (Chapter 4) when that more fundamental change is accomplished. Planning for the replacement retirement system can commence now, however, as the Congress has finally awakened to fixing our country's economic woes.

When a sharpster like Bernie Madoff runs a Ponzi scheme, our community can put him in jail, cluck its collective tongue, intone "Let the buyer beware," and forget it. In the case of Social Security, however, the sharpster was the federal government, which we can't put in jail and then forget it all. Instead we have a joint responsibility, because we haven't been watching Congress and the President closely enough, and we are certainly obligated to do our best to make the victims of the scam as whole as possible. Our whole population is victim, from those not yet working to those retirees presently receiving SS benefits, as detailed below.

The new retirement system, described in considerable detail in Chapter 6 of Ref. 1, will require a new first-time worker to purchase a "BIRA", a Base Income Retirement Annuity, which he will own and will keep as he moves from job to job during his working years. He will never be on the SS roles, and will pay no SS taxes to support anyone else. He determines his own retirement status, had no part in the Ponzi scheme, but will nevertheless have to help pay off SS liabilities via the federal sales tax (Chapter 5) on everyone.

A present worker must select a company offering a BIRA, open the BIRA account, stop paying SS taxes, and start making BIRA premium payments out of his current wages. His previously accumulated SS credits will be converted by the SSA and the BIRA insurance carrier into an equivalent BIRA premium accumulation. That dollar sum will be credited to his BIRA account as an account payable by the government, and will accumulate interest until paid. The government will pay it off over a period of time from its sales tax revenues (Chapter 5), to which the whole population will contribute. Such payments should start with those very close to retirement, so that no new retirees are ever entered onto the SS pension roles.

A present retiree will similarly open a BIRA account into which the government will deposit funds, as it is able, to purchase a single premium life annuity to replace his SS pension, giving him an unchanged retirement income. This procedure will not only shorten the ultimate life of the SS system, but will also act to minimize the cost to the taxpayer of settling these governmental obligations.

This reform of Social Security cannot work or be undertaken until the reforms of the monetary and tax systems (Chapters 4 and 5) are in place, stabilizing the value of the dollar and removing the taxation of investment income. Upon that happy day, however, the actions which Congress must then take to initiate the replacement retirement system are (1) to introduce legislation to define the primary attributes of the retirement system that the Congress recommends to the states that they work with insurance companies to standardize and implement; (2) to require the SSA, and the insurers for all other federally run pension plans, to assist in determining "equivalent BIRA premium accumulations," and then to abolish the SS system and the other federally run pension systems when all their liabilities are paid off; and (3) to fund the government's obligations to pay, over a period of time, its accounts payable to the BIRA accounts of workers and retirees, as described above.

The latter activity being a one-time expense, consideration should be given to paying at least a part of this bill via one-time income events, such as the recovery of taxes on off-the-books dollars in foreign stashes, or the sale of government-owned real property and mineral rights. For example, estimates have been published of trillions of dollars worth of such illegal stashes and more trillions in readily available oil on government-owned land in ANWR, the Arctic National Wildlife Refuge in Alaska.

Attributes of the reformed retirement system are as follows:

1. The system has two primary purposes. The first is to provide for base retirement or long-term disability income for as many retirement-aged or disabled members of our society as possible, to be paid for out of a person's own income during his working years, in order that others will not be burdened for his later upkeep. The second purpose is to make the additional massive pool of capital generated by retirement savings available to the private sector of our economy (not the government!) to promote job creation and economic well-being.

2. The retirement annuity policy that will be created will be paid for and owned by the policy beneficiary, and therefore will be transportable as he moves from job to job (or to unemployment) during his working days. The policy remains in force even if his employer goes out of business.

3. No annuity payout will be available until retirement or the onset of long-term disability, to prevent the dissipation of the account's assets by a profligate worker.

4. No payout will be available to a beneficiary upon the worker's death prior to retirement (the "no refund" clause, as in the SS system).

5. The monthly premiums paid to the insurer will likely vary over the years before retirement. With this functional addition, the annuity policy we have labeled a BIRA, for Base Income Retirement Annuity, is formally defined as a "Flexible Premium Deferred Retirement Annuity Without Refund."

6. A worker's monthly premiums paid into his BIRA must be sufficient to accumulate the capital required to purchase, upon his retirement, an annuity yielding the minimum retirement income specified by state law (e.g., $500 per month). The size of a worker's monthly premium may follow any path through the years that his insurer agrees will produce the required capital on or before the worker's expected retirement date. A wealthy person could purchase a single pay annuity which would grow to the required amount via the company's investments. A low-income person might elect a linearly increasing premium pattern ending with the required accumulation on the person's retirement day. Others may target the required accumulation at other times, for any reason they may have. Whatever the pattern, the company must report annually to the worker whether his payment path remains adequate to reach the required minimum accumulation.

7. The worker may contract with his BIRA insurer for a larger annuity for greater paid premiums. BIRA coverage for other family members should be handled with separate BIRA accounts. Coverages which do not fit the BIRA standard pattern should be separately negotiated with the BIRA issuer or any other insurance company.

8. If a worker and his employer both desire, the worker's premiums may be channeled through his employer via wage deductions, which the employer may arrange for many employees simultaneously if many are so covered.

9. A worker may choose a BIRA insurer irrespective of the state in which that company is incorporated. Further, a worker may diversify by contracting with a second issuer for coverages beyond the base minimum.

10. The terms of the "base" annuity shall be standardized by legal agreement between state lawmakers and insurance companies wishing to participate in this reformed system. The standardization will enable a worker's BIRA policy to be rolled over from one insurer to another, at the volition of the policy owner and the agreement of the new insurer.

11. BIRA policies shall be made available to unemployed, self employed, privately employed, or publicly employed persons, including federal employees.

12. Upon retirement, the worker may pick any fiscally neutral payout options normally available in annuity contracts, such as a Joint Life and Survivorship option.

13. No employer shall be required to pay a BIRA premium for an employee, but nothing shall prevent an employer from voluntarily making such payments as an employment benefit. Some employers may view such payments as an attractive employment incentive, whereas others may find them a significant competitive burden.

14. BIRA policies can readily be adapted to the conversion of retirement annuities offered by private companies, if the companies and their employees so desire.

INDIVIDUAL BENEFITS — MEDICARE

Our Medicare system, initiated with rejoicing and optimism in LBJ's days, has proven to be a monstrous unexpected federal budget hog. The biggest single cause is probably that the public has been conditioned to believe that government *owes* them the best total care. If given the choice between an MRI and an experienced doctor's judgment, they opt for the MRI, since someone else is going to pay for most of that cost. Our fight is to reeducate the public into understanding that *there is no free lunch!*

Our solution parallels that for replacing Social Security. We will create a universally available minimum medical insurance policy called a BMAP, for Base Medical Annuity Policy. While our primary focus is, and should be, on a replacement for the unconstitutional and wildly expensive Medicare system, we shall set about defining a replacement that can readily be extended to a coverage system for workers and others *before* their retirement, though there is nothing constitutionally wrong with such private coverage presently available. Providing medical coverage over a long period of years will give rise to annuitization issues, thereby giving rise to the name BMAP.

Our approach, then, is to describe the more general plan, and then reduce its application to the special case of replacing the Medicare coverage of retirees.

ATTRIBUTES OF THE BMAP SYSTEM ARE:

1. BMAP policies may be taken out by anyone, whether unemployed, self-employed, publicly employed, or privately employed. The policies will provide minimum medical insurance coverage for such persons, and will be required by state law for persons having no insurance or having coverage providing lesser benefits than the BMAP. For higher premium payments, a person can acquire more than the minimum coverage, including coverage for his dependents. His policy will be paid for, owned by, and travel with him from job to job. His employer will not be permitted to purchase the BMAP for him, to avoid his feeling that the coverage is "free," and therefore that "cost is no object" when it comes to selecting medical services.

2. The BMAP will be designed to insure against medical costs that cannot ordinarily be afforded, e.g., heart surgery, and not for office visits and the like. Therefore it will have high annual deductibles and exclusions for very small bills, thereby requiring the owner to pay these small expenses, and giving him an incentive to shop for cheaper options, and avoid services that are not urgently needed.

3.   The minimum BMAP will also have a specified lifetime payment cap, such as $50,000, and no benefits will be paid over that cap amount, to ensure the financial health of the insurer. For larger premium payments the cap may be increased, as the worker so desires and can afford. Similarly, BMAP policies will not grant benefits which are not actuarially justified. A person having a preexisting condition can expect to pay higher than normal premiums, as can an elderly person.

4.   The BMAP will provide for the prepayment by a worker of future medical needs, including temporary periods of unemployment during which his BMAP will stay in force, and of course the expected greater need during retirement years. The policy therefore has an annuity aspect very similar to the BIRA retirement annuity.

5.   The BMAP owner must plan his premium payments not just up to the time of retirement, as in the case with the BIRA, but rather to the end of his life. If retirement is seen as a time of lower income, he may wish for his BMAP premiums to be reduced at that time or perhaps stopped completely. BMAP insurers will annually inform policy owners concerning the amount and sufficiency of their accumulated capital, their accumulations toward policy caps, and other matters which would enable them to make informed decisions concerning altering their coverage or their premium payments.

6.   Congress can recommend to the states the terms of the minimum coverage which should be codified by law into a standard BMAP policy, but the states should work with the insurance companies to reach agreement on the terms, and then codify them in law. The policies should be sufficiently standard so as to enable them to be rolled over from one carrier to another, at the volition of the insured. A person in one state should be permitted to buy a BMAP from a company in any other state.

7.   If a worker switches from his employer's plan to a BMAP, the employer's insurance carrier should figure out the present value of

the worker's present and future coverage, including any retirement medical coverage for which the employer and his carrier are presently liable, and then arrange a transfer of the corresponding assets to the BMAP carrier. Upon that transfer, the worker will be out of Medicare, will stop paying federal Medicare taxes, will consult with his BMAP carrier about a premium payment plan, and will start paying those premiums. When and if all of the employer's workers make this switch, he will then be out of the medical insurance business, but with virtually no impact on either him or his insurance carrier. A worker having arranged such a transfer should not apply to the SSA for Medicare coverage when he retires.

8. If a person already on Medicare switches to BMAP, the Social Security Administration (SSA) administering Medicare will figure out the present value of that person's earned Medicare benefits for which the SSA is liable, and will authorize the Treasury to pay that amount into the person's BMAP account, extinguishing the SSA's liability. The BMAP carrier and the retiree can then consult on the premiums (if any) to be paid during his retirement years.

9. The Medicare liabilities computed above will be paid out of the general revenues of the government, exactly as described in the previous chapter for pension liabilities. Payoff of these liabilities will begin with any working persons having BMAP policies, which will involve payments authorized by the SSA into each individual's BMAP account. When all the workers are paid off, a start should be made on retired persons, budget permitting. When the last of such persons die or are paid off, the federal government will finally be out of the medical insurance business, hopefully forever.

INDIVIDUAL BENEFITS —WELFARE

There are several important problems with the federal welfare system. First, it is in blatant violation of the 10th Amendment, individual welfare not being one of the enumerated powers of the federal government. Second, it tramples the rights of that portion of the citizenry from whom wealth is taken in order to give it to a more favored portion. Buying recipients' votes is obviously in play. Third, the system has created a big underclass of people who have become wards of the nanny state, have recognized that they can survive nicely in that condition, and are perpetuating it with their offspring, and then with the offspring of their offspring. The pattern of families without fathers is sending their male children into crime and prisons, and their female children into prostitution and unmarried single parent "families". The Aid to Families with Dependent Children program is a poster child for bad public policy. LBJ's "War on Poverty" has been lost, with at least as many people in poverty today as there were 40 years ago, in spite of the fruitless expenditure of 6 or 7 trillion dollars, representing a huge part of our present national debt.

Technically speaking, we can easily eliminate this monster of financial waste and societal damage. Political issues are, of course, the obstacles standing in the way. And then we have our New World Order types who may think that massive welfare is one of the corrupt tools to be used in bringing us down. But perhaps, if our economic problems get bad enough, all it will take is a small group of Honest Constitutionalists to convince their legislative cohorts to discard their pandering for votes, and to join them in (1) rounding up and making a list of all the federal welfare programs, including those run by the Department of Health, Education, and Welfare, (2) defunding all of them, and (3) writing the following resolution to the states:

"We have failed in our efforts to make these programs work. Please take them. If you don't like certain of them, discard them. If you see some that might work with some decent local oversight, and which you can afford, you have our blessing to give them your best shot. We have found that trying to administer these programs from thousands of miles away is one of the many reasons we have failed. We recommend that you give county and lower level officials the main authority and responsibility for making your efforts work. Good Luck!

"P.S. Remember that you're trying to create families, help our lower strata to support themselves, and reduce their dependence on society, *not* just make poor people more comfortable.

"P.P.S. Your efforts should include BMAP policies for those who can't yet afford decent medical coverage."

INDIVIDUAL BENEFITS — EDUCATION

Our basic premise concerning education is: the closer the parental control, the better the education. Going from best (closest) to worst (farthest) are the educational entities: private schools selected by parents (with state-issued vouchers), charter schools, public schools, teachers unions, state legislators and bureaucrats, federal legislators and bureaucrats, and lastly the National Education Association (NEA). Since our present subject matter is confined to fixing up what the federal government is doing, the best we can do is to get the federal government entirely out of the education business, with which it has no constitutional authority.

In short, we propose that the Department of Education within HEW, the Department of Health, Education, and Welfare, be abolished, and that any and all remaining interests or obligations of the federal government with respect to education matters (excepting the Veterans Administration) be returned to the several states for them to handle as they see fit, including the granting of educational loans and grants.

FEDERAL LARGESSE —DEPOSIT INSURANCE

Let's take the banking system for our first example. Following the extensive bank failures that occurred in the early thirties, Congress in 1934 passed the first of many unconstitutional deposit insurance measures, covering deposits up to $2,500. The amount covered was increased a number of times in successive years, reaching $100,000 in 1980. By 2010 the limit reached $250,000 for interest bearing accounts and no upper limit for non-interest bearing (checking) accounts. The original insurers were the Federal Deposit Insurance Corporation (FDIC) and the Federal Savings and Loan Insurance Corporation (FSLIC). FSLIC was abolished in 1989 and taken over by the FDIC.

The legislation was originally touted as providing protection for the small depositor, but the $250,000 coverage today goes far beyond small-depositor protection, and is aimed instead at protecting a weak bank by guaranteeing its ability to pay off its short-term liabilities (demand deposits), as was made obvious during the 9/11/2008 banking "crisis" and bailout. The Savings and Loan collapse in the mid-80s gave rise to taxpayer losses of about $125 billion via FSLIC-created liabilities and the FDIC involvement in the resolution process.

Depositors like this federal insurance system, because they no longer have to concern themselves with examining the bank's safety. The weak bankers like it, because they feel safer making risky loans. However, today's FDIC reserves are badly short of the funds to pay off the current list of "troubled" banks, and therefore another monstrous taxpayer bailout is looming, this time of the FDIC itself.

The solution is to institute the 100% reserve system outlined in Chapter 4, which will prevent future runs on banks, and permit the repeal of the FDIC system. That won't happen, however, until a significant Honest Constitutionalist presence is felt in the Congress. In the interim, Congress should announce (1) that the FDIC system will be terminated on a prescribed future date, and that if banks wish to continue a deposit insurance system, they should start now in creating and paying for a private one not dependent upon the taxpayer; and (2) in the event that the private system fails and a given bank is facing bankruptcy, there will be no future infusions of taxpayer funds to forestall that bankruptcy. It can rationally be expected that these measures will rid the banking system of a lot of get-rich-quick operators and replace them with steadier and more prudent banking managers.

FEDERAL LARGESSE —HOUSING

We're going to group in this section the major federal entities having specifically to do with housing. The organizations are HUD, FHA, Fannie May, and Freddie Mac. They are collectively involved with building, selling, financing, and guaranteeing mortgage payments on real estate. They are all unconstitutional, the provision of citizen housing not being one of the enumerated powers of the federal government. As everyone now knows, the federal involvement with housing has recently produced a disastrous taxpayer liability, to say nothing of the ruination of investors around the world, with the big remaining question being, "How can we get out of this mess as cheaply as possible?"

The federal government should sell off all the loans and real estate assets it has acquired through these programs, and terminate the granting of any further loans or loan guarantees, eliminating any additional taxpayer liability. If any states are interested in acquiring any of these assets or programs, they are welcome to them, though it's a little hard to see why a state bureaucracy would be willing to accept these potentially large liabilities.

Note that Chapter 4 on replacing the Fed and creating a banking system having 100% reserves included (item 3) the requirement on any U.S. bank that issues a mortgage that it may sell that mortgage to a third party only if the bank agrees to retain the financial responsibility for servicing that mortgage, including the absorption of any ultimate loss upon its default. This step might also be taken to good effect with the present banking system, i.e., before the Federal Reserve is abolished.

FEDERAL LARGESSE —PBGC

Another category of gratuitously accepted liability is the pension guarantee scheme administered by the Pension Benefit Guarantee Corp., created by the federal government about 35 years ago at the behest of lobbies representing a number of financially precarious companies and their affected workers. We have dealt with this matter in the section above entitled **Individual Benefits – Social Security,** dealing with the replacement of both Social Security and company-based retirement pensions by a private policy called a Base Income Retirement Annuity (BIRA). The BIRA provides workers with retirement pensions which they own, and which stay in force independent of their transfers from employer to employer, or of the financial viability of a given employer. When all workers have been converted to the BIRA system, companies formerly offering retirement pensions will thankfully find themselves out of the retirement business, and the government can then shut down its PBGC business as well, to the benefit of our long-suffering taxpayers.

FEDERAL LARGESSE — FARMING

Still another unconstitutional liability generator has to do with guaranteeing the prices of various farm products. If the price of sugar beets, for example, falls below the federally guaranteed price of X to a world price of Y, the government will pay the farmer the difference, X-Y. This guarantees the farmer's economic prosperity, but at the expense of the taxpayer. Much more properly, sugar and all other farm products are not national treasures, the production of which need subsidizing. Rather, all such farm subsidies should be terminated, relieving the taxpayer of such expenses, and leaving the field open for the private sector handling of the crop insurance business, for which there should be a large demand. With such insurance available, a farmer can take rational account of that expense in his decisions on running his business: how much of which crops should he plant this year, for instance.

Another set of federal farming programs has to do with making farm loans, or guaranteeing farm loans made by others, to farmers who are unable to get financing from commercial sources at normal rates. The U.S. Department of Agriculture is heavy into such high-risk activities, all in violation of the 10th Amendment. These programs should also be brought to an end.

FEDERAL LARGESSE — SBA

The Small Business Administration (SBA) is in the business of making or guaranteeing loans for small business owners who can't find commercial bank loans at normal rates for their projected business activities. The program thus obligates the taxpayer to swallow the default cost of a high-risk loan that commercial lenders want no part of. Our position, of course, is that the federal government's functions should be limited to those enumerated in the Constitution, and not in promoting this business, that business, or any other particular private business. The SBA should be abolished.

FEDERAL LARGESSE — SUMMARY

While we have covered a good number of the major programs granting unconstitutional federal largesse, we believe that many more such programs exist, but our intent should not be mistaken. It is to prohibit U.S.

government bailouts of anyone, foreign or domestic, person or company or country, suffering economic loss or facing bankruptcy, and to abolish, over an appropriate period of time, and while always honoring existing contracts, essentially *all* federal insurance, price guarantee, loan, and loan guarantee programs, none of which are among the enumerated powers of Congress, and hence are in violation of the 10th Amendment.

All of these programs provide or guarantee taxpayer financial support of activities which are judged by the private market to be too risky for it to provide or guarantee. The federal liability for such programs is estimated to have grown to around $5 trillion, representing the rightful obligations of private individuals, groups, or companies which the government has been somehow persuaded to assume in the name of the U.S. taxpayer. If any such program is nevertheless deemed important enough to maintain, it should be made the subject of a constitutional amendment, where the bulk of the states and their voters would have a say in the matter. The Price-Anderson bill, which caps the liability of nuclear power plant operators, would be one such candidate.

MISCELLANEOUS — FDA

The U.S. Food and Drug Administration (FDA) says this about itself on its website:

"The FDA is responsible for protecting the public health by assuring the safety, efficacy, and security of human and veterinary drugs, biological products, medical devices, our nation's food supply, cosmetics, and products that emit radiation, and by regulating the manufacture, marketing, and distribution of tobacco products.

"The FDA is also responsible for advancing the public health by helping to speed innovations that make medicines and foods more effective, safer, and more affordable; and helping the public get the accurate, science-based information they need to use medicines and foods, and to reduce tobacco use to improve health."

These two paragraphs contain a long list of functions which are not constitutionally enumerated, as evidenced by the phrases assuring efficacy, regulating manufacture, speed innovations, more affordable, improve health, etc. One of the most egregious of these functions is assuring the efficacy of drugs. This is the item which has given rise to the FDA's hugely expensive testing requirements for new drugs which only the large pharmaceutical companies can afford, with smaller firms being driven out of the field. It has become impossible to bring a new pharmaceutical product to market without a big price tag, earning the FDA the sobriquet "the unconstitutional birthplace of high prescription costs." The function of "efficacy" should be removed from the FDA's purview, along with the bulk of the remaining listed functions.

The only possible exception is "assuring the safety of our nation's food and drug supplies," based upon a stretch of the "General Welfare" clause in the first sentence of Article I Section 8. The rest of the listed functions should be defunded and returned to the states to do with as they wish.

MISCELLANEOUS —BUSINESS REGULATION

There is no enumerated power permitting Congress to write law aimed at regulating what category of person a company can or cannot hire (sex, race, age, education, prior experience, etc.); permissible working conditions (hours, wages, safety, working environment, etc.); business matters (prices, profits, dividends, subsidies, etc.); or what entities (including the federal government) may own shares or otherwise control the operation of a business. The federal government's recent bailout and acquisition of a managerial share of several automobile and insurance companies was utterly without Constitutional foundation, and therefore in violation of the 10th Amendment. (See paragraph on Constitutional Authority below.)

Any existing law regulating the unenumerated activities listed in the above paragraph should be repealed, such as the federal minimum wage law.

MISCELLANEOUS — AUTHORITY DELEGATION

Consider the following two federal agencies:

EPA – Environmental Protection Agency

OSHA - Occupational Safety and Health Administration

These agencies were created by the Congress and given a *general mandate* to define what was needed to be done and then to enforce their findings. The agencies were not only charged with pursuing unenumerated goals, and therefore in violation of the 10th Amendment, but in addition were unconstitutionally granted legislative, executive, and judicial powers. They could thus define the rules, enforce them, and deliver punishments to the guilty. Not surprisingly, the agencies became despotic, and came to be feared almost as much as the IRS, the poster child of such agencies. The power to delegate the legislative authority of Congress to other agencies is certainly not an enumerated power granted to Congress by the Constitution.

Environmental and occupational safety issues are functions which many states have themselves dealt with, the appropriate action therefore being to defund these federal agencies and transfer their functions to the individual states for them to do with as they wish. Congress could profitably go through the several top layers of the entire Executive Branch, listing other agencies making and enforcing all their own rules, and getting rid of them, saving lots of taxpayer dollars at every step.

MISCELLANEOUS — UNIVERSALITY

Congressmen have fallen heavily into the trap of "bringing home the bacon" for their constituents. The bacon almost always has to do with an expenditure benefiting some or all of a congressman's constituents in a particular town, county, or state at the expense of all citizens outside of that particular area. This taking of one person's property (his tax money) and giving it to another to whom it did not belong is close to the dictionary definition of plunder, but because it is being done under the cover of law, it should more accurately be labeled "legal plunder."

Many congressmen justify these actions by noting that "everyone else is doing it" and so look for ways to enhance their corrupt efforts, rather than terminate them. Thus was born the process of "logrolling," meaning, "I'll vote for your goodies if you vote for mine," thereby acknowledging the moral muck that the whole Congress is stuck in.

If one peruses the enumerated powers in Article I Section 8, the universality of the permitted legislative activities becomes obvious. Consistent with this observation, the following constitutional amendment is proposed:

Congress shall make no law respecting any organization, product, or service the functioning of which does not benefit substantially equally the citizens of each of the United States.

Application of this amendment will return the responsibility for unique state and local needs back to the state and local governments, where the responsibility belongs.

MISCELLANEOUS — CONSTITUTIONAL AUTHORITY

In the heat of political battle, congressional legislators frequently seek to pass legislation which may appear to them to solve immediate problems, but which the founders would have deemed highly unwise. Those founders did their best to prevent such laws from being created by wording the Constitution to explicitly limit the functions which the federal government would be permitted to address. The Congress has nevertheless gone far astray, with the disastrous results which we can all see. This chapter has listed a large number of these missteps and our proposals to repair the damage.

To help prevent future missteps of this kind, Congress should introduce and pass a constitutional amendment, and deliver it to the states for their ratification, requiring Congress to include in the opening words of every bill sent to the President for his approval the constitutional authority permitting the creation of that bill. Without such stated authority, the bill shall be deemed void.

If the Congress, later laboring under such a constitutional restriction, feels that some particular bill, not having such constitutional authority, absolutely must be passed, then Congress should introduce and pass a constitutional amendment authorizing the subject of their concern to be permitted. That is, it should use the mechanism which the founders included in Article V of the Constitution to enable the Constitution to be amended when the motivation for so doing was strong enough.

Chapter 9

Apply Checks & Balances

The Constitution was deliberately designed by our founders to keep despotic power from being accumulated in any one branch of the federal government. Therefore they gave "balanced" portions of the total federal power to each of the legislative, executive, and judicial branches. Each branch was also given certain powers to "check" the operations of the other two branches if one or another of them appeared to be engaged in an unconstitutional or unauthorized activity.

All the members of all the branches are sworn to uphold the Constitution. Under a future regime of Honest Constitutionalism, all elective legislative and executive members and all executive and judicial members appointed and confirmed by the Senate will know that all other members of those groups will have been truth-tested and given a Truth in Politics Certificate, as described in Chapter 3. But until that happy day, we know that a good number of such members of the three branches will have taken their oaths of office with their fingers crossed behind their backs. The founders also knew that that situation would arise, and so created constitutional checks to try to keep the federal government on a straight and narrow path

The functions of the legislative, executive, and judicial branches are, respectively, to make the laws, execute the laws, and to judge conflicts which arise upon the application of the laws. The reality of today's problem (i.e., in early 2011) is that the three branches have become grossly unbalanced, with both the judicial and executive branches exercising rights that the Constitution has reserved to the legislative branch. The Congress has the constitutional power to rein in the usurpers, but doesn't apparently have enough members who even care about the problem, at least more than the problem of staying in office, to make use of that power. The Congress has in fact pretty much accepted the role of passing the laws requested by the executive, rather than the more difficult role of creating constitutional laws by their own initiative and in response to the wishes of their constituents.

The primary powers which the Constitution gives to Congress to check any unconstitutional actions of the executive and judicial branches are:

1. The House has the sole power to impeach (Art. I, Sect. 2) the President, the VP, and all civil officers of the U.S. (Art. II, Sect. 4), which certainly includes the cabinet officers and judges confirmed by the Senate.

2. The Senate has the sole power to try all impeachments (Art. I, Sect. 3).

3. An offending officer, upon impeachment for and conviction of treason, bribery, or other high crimes and misdemeanors, shall be removed from office (Art. II, Sect. 4).

4. The Senate has the sole power to ratify treaties signed by the President and to ratify the appointments of judges and executive officers (Art. II, Sect. 2).

5. The Supreme Court has appellate jurisdiction of all cases (excepting those involving ambassadors and other ministers) "with such exceptions, and under such regulations, as the Congress shall make" (Art. III, Sect. 2).

6. All bills for raising revenue must originate in the House (Art. I, Sect. 7), and no money may be drawn from the Treasury except as authorized by a legal Appropriation (Art. I, Sect. 9) thus giving the House the power to defund any portion of a law as it may wish.

The Supreme Court offends by writing new "law" as a part of a judgment, as we shall illustrate. The executive offends by similarly writing "law" via executive orders, or by deciding what portion of a law passed by Congress, sometimes over a presidential veto, will be enforced by the executive, as we shall also illustrate.

The issue of abortion goes on and on because the Supreme Court in 1973, by its *Roe v. Wade* ruling, made new "law" (an unconstitutional act) instead of sending the case back to the Texas court with a much narrower ruling on the specific case. The new law which the court made defined which abortions were legal and which were not. That new law can't itself be repealed or voted upon by the Congress, because making law covering medical procedures on citizens is not one of the enumerated powers of the Congress, and would be in violation of the 10th Amendment. Thus the Supreme Court not only went beyond its judicial powers by making a new "law," but also the law that it made was itself unconstitutional.

The situation could be rectified by the Supreme Court reversing itself, but instead of waiting, the Congress should have taken action at the time, and still can. Congress, recognizing that the Supreme Court has overreached its authority, has the power (Article III, Section 2) to nullify the court's ruling by passing a resolution denying the Supreme Court jurisdiction in cases involving abortion, and to simultaneously acknowledge the lack of constitutional authority for Congress itself to legislate in this field, in consonance with the 10th Amendment of the Constitution. These actions will have the effect of returning the authority to the several states to legislate as they will concerning abortion, legally returning the country to the approximate condition that existed before the *Roe v. Wade* decision.

A current example of the President's failure to perform his constitutional duty to "...faithfully execute the office of President of the United States" (Art. II, Sect. 1) is his failure to enforce the laws presently on the books outlawing illegal immigration, notwithstanding the entreaties from several southern border states for the President to enforce those laws and/or to authorize the states to do so.

What would a Congress of Honest Constitutionalists do? It would introduce the state authorization law requested by the states. If that failed to be passed and signed by the President, it would demand that the President and his Attorney General vigorously enforce the existing law. Lacking their positive response, it would institute impeachment proceedings against the President, his refusal to act being in violation of his constitutional duty to "...take care that the laws be faithfully executed" (Art. II, Sect. 3). His ignoring this primary constitutional duty is about as high a constitutional crime as a President can commit.

Similarly, if the President includes a "signing statement" along with his signature approving a bill, and the Congress takes strong exception to that act as a deliberate infringement of its constitutional prerogatives, it clearly has the option of proceeding down the impeachment path. By so doing, Congress would be declaring, "We are no longer Junior Partners. *We* decide what the laws are, and you have the job of enforcing them. If there are parts of a law you don't like, ask us to modify the law, and we will entertain your request."

"Executive Orders" have recently become a common device to get around a slow or recalcitrant Congress. When such orders involve massive changes in policy, or major expenditure of taxpayer money, they should most assuredly be vigorously opposed as an infringement of Congress' powers, justifying the congressional actions of defunding or impeachment. The recent bombing of Serbia and the First Gulf War come to mind, both preemptive and lacking the constitutional declaration of war required by Art. I, Sect. 8.

Chapter 10

Destroy Illegal Drug Trade

Chapter 11 of Ref. 1 sketched out our domestic drug problem and the federal "solution" – the creation of a Drug Enforcement Agency (DEA) under whose auspices we have mounted a "War on Drugs." About $5 billion per year has been expended on this effort, to little or no effect, but which is as *nothing* compared to the several hundred billion dollar loss each year associated with drug dollars leaving the country. Added to this are our drug-spawned crime losses, including legal and incarceration costs, to say nothing of the monstrous cost of the trauma and the lowered productivity which this social horror has brought upon our whole people.

Ref. 1 concludes, however, that even if we can't stop high-priced illegal drugs at their source, or at our borders, or before delivery to our kids on the street, we certainly can accomplish our main goals of eliminating both the social trauma and the crime costs associated with drugs by dealing with them in essentially the same way we deal with alcohol and tobacco: we legalize them, or as some would say, we medicalize them.

In more detail, we propose that legal paths be established within a given state via which medically certified addicts resident in that state may obtain the drugs they need in order to function as employed, tax-paying citizens of that state. The drugs should be sold in stores licensed by the given state via prescription from a physician licensed to perform that function. The cost to the addict should reflect only the market cost to the pharmacist of obtaining the drugs from legal sources. Those sources should include any state licensed entities able to supply cheap drugs of controlled purity and potency, and capable of satisfying the addict's needs. Substitute drugs may play a role, such as methadone, or any other substitutes that may be developed.

Along with the delivery of such legal drugs, information should be copiously supplied to the addict that will help him get off of drugs completely. Further, we propose that the various states budget funds to mount educational campaigns aimed at our youth to teach them about the downside of drug addiction, with at least the intensity of the programs aimed at getting people to quit smoking.

Very importantly, we should at the same time rescind the search and seizure laws that were promulgated in the name of the drug war, laws which have sometimes permitted warrantless searches and the seizure and sale of personal property even before a person has been formally charged with a crime. Such gross constitutional violations simply have no place in the life of a free society, and the offending laws should presently be repealed. Specifically, Congress should:

1. Repeal laws proscribing the sale or use of narcotic drugs on the federal "controlled substance" list.

2. Repeal authorization of the federal DEA, and announce the termination of the federal War on Drugs.

3. Repeal all federal search and seizure laws that were enacted in support of the War on Drugs.

4. Create and deliver to the state legislatures for their consideration a model state law enabling addicts resident in the given state to obtain narcotic drugs cheaply and legally, including marijuana, methamphetamine, and any other lesser drugs that the state may wish. The new law may be applied by the Congress itself to the District of Columbia, per Article I, Section 8.

With this program in place, the federal government will have removed itself from the illegal drug suppression business. The addict's cost of supporting a heroin or coke addiction should tumble to perhaps one or two percent of its former cost, making the illegal drug trade unprofitable. The trade will then disappear, including importers, street pushers, and money launderers. The number of new addicts each year will become residually small. Crime related to these hard drugs will substantially disappear, and our prison populations will drastically decline. We will be relieved of huge financial losses, measured in part by the river of drug cash which is now flowing out of the country into worldwide off-the-books accounts. We will also be relieved of the $5 billion annual cost of the War on Drugs.

Why hasn't such a program been started long ago? Because the profits from the drug trade are one of the primary sources of funding for the illicit actions of the oligarchy in promoting their New World Order program. In a word, their War on Drugs is really a war on the American middle class. Chapter 9 of Ref. 2 is devoted to detailing the CIA involvement in the Vietnamese War, its promotion of opium production in the Golden Triangle area, and the establishment of labs producing heroin for the worldwide market, including the U.S. Chapter 9 (p. 199) states, "The United States had just fought a war which had produced, with our complicity, the greatest illicit heroin production and delivery network that the world has ever seen, and that the population of the United States was the primary targeted market."

It then goes into a discussion of the war in Afghanistan, by which the CIA managed the political maneuvering which brought that country into full production of opium and the delivery of that opium to the heroin labs in neighboring Pakistan. It supplies some details, as follows (p. 200):

> The United States was involved in a second anti-Communist war run covertly by the CIA which resulted in the development of a second major heroin production area, rivaling the Golden Triangle. The war lasted from 1979 to 1989. The battleground was Afghanistan. The Communist threat was supplied by Russia. The CIA client was the neighboring country of Pakistan, specifically in the persons of General Zia ul-Haq, who was newly running the country following a military coup, and his chosen Afghan guerrilla client, Gulbuddin Hekmatyar. Hekmatyar ended up being the enforcer for opium production in the neighboring Afghan highlands, plus its collection and delivery to heroin labs in Pakistan, all under the protection of General Zia, and using arms supplied by the CIA and American "military aid."

The origins of the above conflict are interesting. In April 1978, Communist elements in the Afghan army had thrown out the previous dictator and established a pro-Soviet regime. Then in April 1979 Zbigniew Brzezinski, President Carter's National Security Advisor and conduit to our elites, convinced the National Security Council to be "more sympathetic" to the fledgling anti-Communist resistance. A month later, a CIA special envoy arrived in Pakistan to interview Afghan resistance leaders, and selected Hekmatyar, the man recommended by Pakistan's Inter-

Service Intelligence agency, through which General Zia intended to prosecute the upcoming conflict. A half-year later, Russia invaded Afghanistan. President Carter made a public display on TV denouncing Leonid Brezhnev, and sent Brzezinski out again to twist some arms and rustle up some arms for the resistance. He got them, from China, Egypt, and Saudi Arabia, plus of course some from the CIA itself. President Reagan later followed up with a $3 billion program of military aid to Pakistan.

Then Chapter 11 of Ref. 2 goes into excruciating detail concerning the people and organizations involved in handling drug money, from cash sales recycled by complicit banks to poppy-growing farmers, to financing the production of heroin from the poppies, to delivery to target countries and sales to their addicts, and to laundering and distributing the proceeds, some to the NWO operators, some to official bribery, and some being recycled to the poppy farmers for the next year's crop. The oligarchs clearly don't want to give up this lucrative trade. Ref. 2 (pp. 288-289), in reviewing "Dope, Inc." by the Executive Intelligence Review (EIR), has this to say about banks managing illicit money off of their regular books:

> Back in the early 60's, the First National City Bank had hired a Dutchman, Robert Meyjes, who proposed to set up a "private international banking" division of the bank. He did so, and sent some 600 bank trainees through the division in the next 10 years. Meyjes is now in Citibank's Paris office, and his "trainees" are scattered in various banks around the world, running an "old-boy" network of covert "banking," privately handling the deposits of people who are not anxious to say where their money came from. David Rockefeller's Chase Manhattan Bank quickly caught on (they referred to it internally as "looking for Mafia money"), and followed suit, not very successfully, says the EIR, until they accepted onto their board Mr. Y.K. Pao, the vice-chairman of the HongShang [the Hong Kong and Shanghai Bank], prior to which they found no entry into Hong Kong's lucrative activities.

Ref. 2 (p. 301) summarizes as follows:

Two other major areas may be attacked, as suggested by the EIR. One is money laundering, though we believe that as street distribution declines following drug "medicalization," fewer dollars will require laundering, making detection that much more difficult. Special attention should be given, however, to "private international banking" adjuncts to domestic banks, as described by the EIR, and laws aimed at preventing illicit funds from being deposited should be strengthened.

The last major area to be attacked, if we really wish to get serious, involves an attack on the overall drug system, utilizing laws presently on the books against criminal syndicalism. We should bring to clear public attention the roles being played by the Golden Triangle countries, Afghanistan, Communist China, the Hong Kong heroin labs, the HongShang, the RIIA and CFR, Mexico, the Cali Cartel, the Bronfmans, the U.S. mobs in their employ, the "rogue" British financial institutions controlling these elements, and their American subsidiaries. Americans suspected of being involved in the syndicate, whether overtly engaged in banking, government (e.g., the CIA), or local crime, should be publicly charged and tried. Without such public exposure, the American public is unlikely to rouse itself sufficiently to even support the "medicalization" program discussed above.

Note the importance of the last two sentences above. Americans won't accept medicalization unless they are convinced of the urgency of the drug threat. That urgency will be imparted upon the public's learning about the criminal banking and governmental participation in the illegal drug trade. Therefore, given the requisite Honest Constitutionalist strength, Congress should:

1. Create a congressional committee to formally investigate which major domestic institutions, private or public, financial or otherwise, are or have been handling drug money originating in the U.S., and who own the accounts into which such money has been deposited. Special attention should be given to "private international banking" units created to handle off-the-books deposits. Hold public hearings to display to the public the

ongoing investigation, to question alleged wrongdoers, and to otherwise lay the groundwork for prosecution.

2. Publish the results of the investigation, particularly identifying the foreign sources of narcotic drugs and the identity of individuals, organizations, and countries covertly supporting such production. Distribute the investigative results both to the U.S. public and throughout the world, to aid other countries in their efforts to exterminate the drug trade in their own countries.

3. Introduce any new law that the investigation has shown may be needed to strengthen existing law regarding drug trafficking and drug money laundering.

4. Request the President and his Attorney General to initiate the prosecution of the alleged wrongdoers.

5. Prosecute, fine, and incarcerate the CEOs and board members of banks found guilty of laundering drug money, and fine such banks severely enough to jolt their stockholders or private owners.

6. Prosecute, fine, and incarcerate the owners of the off-the-books accounts found to be holding illicit (untaxed) funds. Disgorge such funds from the institutions holding them, and appropriate them to pay down the U.S. national debt.

7. Prosecute, fine, and incarcerate the managers and owners of companies found guilty of transporting drugs into or within the United States, and freeze and confiscate the material and financial assets of such companies.

8. Prosecute, fine, and incarcerate government operatives found guilty of managing, facilitating, or withholding their knowledge of the drug trade being used for government agency purposes, especially including law enforcement, military, and intelligence agencies.

9. If the President blocks by his action or inaction any or all of the four prosecutions listed above, apply the check on his malfeasance provided by the Constitution, namely impeachment, as described in Chapter 9 above.

Chapter 11

Fix Immigration System

The basic idea behind our historical system of immigration control was (1) to welcome those who knew about our primary civic goal of freedom and who wished to assimilate and participate in that quest, but (2) to exclude those who would maintain their original allegiances or otherwise become societal liabilities, e.g., criminals or parasites.

Our prosperity relative to the rest of the world has encouraged the do-gooders among us to welcome any category of immigrant who is less fortunate, for whatever the reason, resulting in floods of people surging across our sieve-like borders without the technicality of asking permission. They then take advantage of state services that are legally or illegally available to them, including helping near-term pregnant women to have citizen-babies born in the U.S. Complicit politicians garner (illegal) votes from these groups, and complicit employers use them as a source of cheap labor. Other well-connected groups will use their group strength to undermine our political processes in support of their own agendas.

Our society is suffering badly by the growth of these unassimilable groups, by our acceptance of our violated rule of law, by the growing financial burden of delivering social services to these groups, and by the growing lack of cohesion within our society. Societally speaking, cohesion is a much greater virtue than diversity. Secret societies and secret agendas are our enemies, and honesty and openness are our sought-for virtues.

When an Honest Constitutionalist Congress comes on the scene, here is what it should do:

1. Enact a constitutional amendment to modify Section 1 of the 14th Amendment to grant citizenship to a baby born in the United States only if each parent is provably a US citizen. "Provably" means tendering to a county clerk or other official a birth certificate or other acceptable proof of citizenship. If the requisite proof is presented, the birth certificate will be issued indicating citizen status for the newborn. Otherwise, the certificate will be

issued indicating non-citizen status.

2. Enact law requiring that legal entry of an alien, on either a temporary or permanent basis, should be preceded by the delivery of documentation to the INS concerning the identity of the subject, including birth certificates or other documents certifying the subject's date and place of birth and the identity of his/her parents. Photographs and fingerprints will be taken at the time of application for entry. Copies of these materials, plus an INS identity number, the visa type, the date, time, and place of admission, and the visa expiration date shall be included on an "INS Identity Card" which will be delivered to the applicant upon entry to enable the later sure verification of identity by employers or local authorities. An applicant staying in the country beyond his temporary visa's expiration date will thereafter be treated as an illegal immigrant.

3. If the applicant is applying for entry to perform temporary agricultural labor, the visa type will be shown as H-2A. The use of this visa type should be encouraged to the extent that farmers need this source of labor for the successful operation of their farms. To reduce the farmer's incentives to hire illegal immigrants who are generally willing to work for very small wages and benefits, enact law reducing the cost to employers of hiring legal H-2A visa holders. Specifically:

   (a) Exempt H-2A visa holders from the federal minimum wage law (if it still exists. See Chap. 8, Miscellaneous – Business Regulation),

   (b) Permit the automatic limited extension of an H-2A worker's entry period upon the written request of his agricultural employer, and

   (c) Ask the states to remove the requirement for the employer to pay worker compensation premiums for the H-2A worker, but to let the worker pay the premiums if he wishes to have the coverage.

4. The laws presently in place prohibiting the employment of illegal aliens and prescribing penalties for violations must be strictly enforced. Employers are presently required by federal law to fill out an "I-9 form" on each new employee, containing the data needed to satisfy the legal requirements for employment, including citizenship data, etc. Further, a legal H-2A worker should have his INS-issued identification card with him, making it easy for the employer to identify and refuse employment to those who cannot prove their legal status. The employer should then be required, under penalty of law, to report to the INS the contact information on job applicants who were unable to supply proof of citizenship or all the required I-9 data.

5. Enact federal law denying the granting of any federally funded public service to an illegal immigrant, and permitting states to similarly deny state funded services. The services in question are taxpayer supported health, education, and welfare services (delivered by hospitals, schools, and welfare agencies), and specifically include voter registration services. To receive any such service, the applicant must tender proof of citizenship (e.g., birth certificate, passport, or proof of naturalization), or, if citizenship is not claimed, documented verification from the INS of permanent alien resident status, before the service, if the law permits, will be delivered. The only service to be excepted from service denial shall be emergency medical service for an immediate life-threatening condition. The service agency shall also be required, under penalty of law, to inform the INS of the identity of immigrant applicants unable to supply proof of citizenship or permanent alien residency.

6. Enact federal law permitting state and local agencies to assist the Immigration and Naturalization Service (INS) in identifying, apprehending, holding, and delivering suspect illegal immigrants within the state to the INS for investigation, and in assisting in their deportation if such is ordered.

7. Enact model state law, applicable to DC, and delivered to the

several states for their consideration, to charge and prosecute persons within the jurisdiction of the state for financing or otherwise assisting illegal immigrants to enter the country, to obtain citizenship or permanent resident alien status, to find employment, or to claim any taxpayer-subsidized health, education, welfare, or other benefit which the law does not explicitly permit.

8. Pass federal law requiring the immediate deportation of any illegal immigrant found guilty of a felony, and the expeditious deportation of any immigrant unable to prove lawful entry and residence within 30 days of detainment.

9. Hold congressional hearings to expose and publicize the criminal movement called La Raza (see Ref. 5) by Mexican legal and illegal immigrants to return the southwest portion of the United States to Mexican ownership and/or control. Enact new law as the hearings may find desirable. Identify, impeach, and try any American officials suspected of giving aid and comfort to this movement. Identify, arrest, and prosecute other American and foreign individuals or organizations for giving financial support or other aid and comfort to this movement. American citizens found guilty of treason or aiding illegal immigration should be punished in accordance with applicable law. Non-citizen individuals and organizations found guilty shall be deported and suffer the confiscation of all personal and organizational assets. If the Executive refuses to execute these prosecutions, apply the congressional check of impeaching the President.

10. Increase the INS funding and demand that the funding be utilized to accomplish the above actions. If the Executive refuses or procrastinates, see Chapter 9 on Checks and Balances.

Chapter 12

Avoid Foreign Entanglements

George Washington's famous Farewell Address, never delivered as a speech, but first printed on September 26, 1796 and widely printed thereafter, announced his decision to decline a third term of office as President. He then used the occasion to adjure his readers (a) to assure that the Constitution be sacredly maintained, and utilized with wisdom and virtue; (b) to cherish the unity of the new national Union, it being the main pillar supporting the people's independence, tranquility, peace, safety, prosperity, and highly prized Liberty; (c) to resist factions opposing the Constitution or undermining it by misinterpreting its principles [the clauses regarding general welfare and interstate commerce come to mind]; (d) to beware the actions of political parties, each of which will tend to seek corrupt power in order to dominate the other; (e) to carefully preserve, and modify by constitutional amendment as needed, the checks on one governmental branch by another; (f) to respect, maintain, and cherish the moral strictures of religion as the "firmest props of the duties of Men and Citizens"; (g) to promote institutions for the diffusion of knowledge, it being essential that public opinion be enlightened; and (h) to protect the country's credit by spending sparingly, cultivating peace, and taxing as needed to avoid accumulating debt to be paid by our posterity.

The rest of the address, about one-third of the whole, is devoted to the issue of avoiding foreign entanglements. The theory behind this position is simple: We don't want some other country to involve itself in our country's affairs, and we should respect them by not involving our country in their affairs. We should be prepared to defend ourselves from attack, but should not be involved with defending or attacking someone else. Washington applied this principle during his own administration by declaring neutrality at the start of the Napoleonic era in Europe, keeping us out of that European war, and permitting our own country to continue its peaceful growth toward self-sufficiency.

For a whole century after Washington delivered these words, they were adhered to reasonably well by those who followed. During the last century, however, violations of his advice have repeatedly been made, with the results today (early 2011) being national bankruptcy, a looming depression, and the hatred of much of the world. The rest of this chapter consists of rehearsing a number of these violations, our goal being to strengthen Congress' will to adhere to Washington's admonitions. The list will include the Spanish-American War, World War I, World War II, the Korean War, the Vietnam War, the Israeli-Palestinian War, the First Iraq War, the Afghan War, the Second Iraq War, and the incipient wars against Pakistan and Iran.

1. The Spanish-American War

This was the 1898 war against Spain in which the U.S. took the side of Cuban and Philippine revolutionaries, defeated Spain in a four-month war, and took temporary possession of Cuba, the Philippines, Puerto Rico, and Guam. President McKinley tried to avoid the war, but was opposed by investors in Cuban sugar, by William Randolph Hearst's *New York Journal*, and by Joseph Pulitzer's *New York World*, all of them leading public opinion toward supporting the downtrodden revolutionaries. McKinley sent an emissary to Spain to help reach a settlement, but later sent the battleship *Maine* to Havana to protect allegedly threatened American interests.

On February 15 the ship suffered a massive explosion and sank in Havana harbor. (Upon the much later investigation by the famed U.S. Admiral Hyman Rickover, he concluded that the explosion occurred internally, not from an external mine.) The public was outraged, Congress passed and McKinley signed a resolution demanding Spanish withdrawal from Cuba and authorizing the President to use force to that end. The resolution was sent to Spain, which treated it as an ultimatum and on April 21 broke diplomatic relations. The U.S. then instituted a naval blockade of Cuba, Spain declared war on April 23, and the Congress declared that a state of war had existed since the blockade had started on April 21.

During the preceding century, the world oligarchy centered in London had destroyed the strong governments of France, Austria, and Italy, and had begun working on undermining Germany. The Spanish-American War would now destroy the last vestiges of a Spanish Empire, the new twist being that U.S. military power would be used for that purpose, it being close to the desired point of attack (Cuba). Manipulating the U.S. people and their government into doing the hard lifting for them was child's play for the oligarchs: use the controlled press to generate sympathy for the oppressed, greed over future sugar profits, rationalization for intervention, and finally outrage over a (phony) attack on a U.S. battleship. The bamboozled American people quitted the war with a smug feeling of contentment concerning their successful entry into the world of internationalism, setting them up for the much more serious ventures that the oligarchy had in store for them.

2. World War I

This war was brought into existence by the efforts of Queen Victoria's first-born, Edward VII, for 40 years the Prince of Wales, and finally King of England upon the death of his mother. Edward himself died in 1910, but had worked the previous 20 years to surround Germany with his military alliances. His plan was taken up by his successors, and in 1914 the fuse was lit and World War I, "the war to end all wars," was started. (See Ref. 3, pp. 262-271.) By the third year of the war, England was facing defeat (by starvation brought on by German U-boats), and to stave off the defeat made a deal with World Zionism to give the Zionists a homeland in Palestine in return for their help in bringing the U.S. into the war to defeat Germany.

The plan worked, but in the process Trotsky and his band were transported from New York to and through Germany and into Russia, where they successfully mounted the 1917 Russian Revolution, conquering the Russian state and bringing overt militant communism into the world. Germany was defeated, with Versailles setting the stage for the next big war. The Balfour Declaration was announced, and the Jewish migration from Europe into Palestine began. (See Ref. 2, pp. 6-7 and 108-111.)

As with the Spanish-American War, the U.S. public was against going to war (Wilson ran in 1916 declaring his opposition to the war). But when the value of British war bonds was threatened, and the Zionist agreement was secretly made, and memory of the (secretly planned) 1915 *Lusitania* sinking was brought again to the public, and the Morgan interests turned up the tempo for war via their purchased editorial rights in the nation's big papers, Wilson changed his tune, the public patriotically responded, and Congress, violating Washington's warnings, declared war.

3. World War II

After Versailles, and the oligarch's failure to get America to join their League of Nations, they started planning for the next war. But first they took some time off to further enrich themselves by creating a bubble of banking credit ("the roaring 20's"), selling out, pricking the bubble on August 9, 1929, and buying the good stuff back at the market bottom. (See Ref. 2, pp. 114-118.) Then they returned to the business of war.

To have a good war, you must have credible enemies. The Bank of England saw to the financing of Hitler, and FDR recognized the USSR and otherwise helped it along (secretly) by filling his various commissions and bureaus with communist sympathizers, who Truman, a dozen years later, struggled to get rid of. As with the previous two wars, the public didn't want it, and FDR repetitiously intoned, "I hate war." However, once reelected in 1940, he and Winston Churchill plotted to get Japan, with its highly useful military alliance with Hitler, to attack Pearl Harbor.

Germany of course was the primary target, and Japan was the "patsy" used to get the war started. FDR kept the Pearl Harbor commanders in the dark, even as he monitored the progress of the Japanese fleet across the Pacific, getting in position to launch its air attack. Warnings of the upcoming event, including the date and place of the attack, came to Washington from many other countries around the world which had sniffed out Japanese plans, but FDR ignored them all, and persisted in his treason. (See Ref. 4, p. 64.)

The attack and the subsequent war came off very nicely, even including a formal, publicly backed declaration of war against Japan and Germany, with the establishment media complicit to this day with the coverup. The war, hugely expensive in dollars and lives, produced the United Nations that World War I failed to produce, and our country thereafter had the internationalist United Nations to guide us as to how we should spend our dollars, which wars we should help fight, etc.

4. The Korean War

The Russo-Japanese War of 1904 was fought over the issue of exclusive control over Manchuria, desired by Russia, and exclusive control over Korea, desired by Japan. Japan won the war, with the Russians suing for peace in order to give its full attention to its own 1905 revolution. The 1905 peace treaty gave Japan control over Korea, which would be annexed to Japan by the 1910 Japan-Korea Annexation Treaty. Thirty-five years later, the World War II winners (USSR and USA) agreed, though opposed by most Koreans, to split Korea at the 38th parallel, administer the two parts under a UN trusteeship, hold an election aimed at restoring a single government, and depart. They backed opposing candidates, however, and were soon at war.

That decision to involve the U.S. in Korean affairs led to a serious shooting war with communist clients of the USSR, and very closely to an actual invasion of Communist China. Sixty years later, with an armistice still in force, the U.S. is still maintaining troops in South Korea, waiting on tenterhooks for another hot war with North Korea, which is presently identified by current American leaders as a member of an "Axis of Evil" opposing us. The reality of the Korean split is that neither the U.S. nor the USSR wants to militarily fight each other over Korea, and our oligarchs are apparently satisfied to just keep the issue simmering and economically bleeding us from yet one more of a thousand cuts.

5. The Vietnam War

In discussing the illegal drug trade in Chapter 10, we noted the CIA involvement in the Vietnam War, its promotion of opium production in the Golden Triangle area, and the establishment of labs producing heroin for the worldwide market, including the U.S. In fact, as far back as 1955, the American CIA and the French military were in an unheralded war, using proxies on both sides, for the control of Saigon and South Vietnam. Why? Because the French were already using the drug trade in that area to support their own secret intelligence services, and the CIA wanted it all. (See Ref. 2, pp. 187-188.) The CIA won, and in the decade to follow set about to consolidate and grow their (illegal) drug franchise. A real war in the area would help to conceal their activities and give them additional time to develop the manufacture, transport, and other elements of their enterprise.

Fortunately for them, an evil ogre was on the horizon, moving down from North Vietnam, by name the Communist Pathet Lao. Even before John Kennedy's death, and during the early months of LBJ's term, American "advisors" were giving aid and comfort to the South, about which the Nasty

Northern Communists objected. Then came the critical event.

A number of North Vietnamese torpedo boats allegedly attacked the American destroyer *USS Maddox*, which returned fire. No American was hurt, and no floating signs of damage were later found. Argument persists to this day about whether such an attack actually existed at all, or if it did, who was responsible for initiating it. It resulted, however, in LBJ writing, and the Congress approving on August 7, 1964 by wide margins, the Gulf of Tonkin Resolution, by which the Congress, without a formal declaration of war, "authorized" the President to take any action necessary to assist any member of the Southeast Asia Collective Defense Treaty, meaning South Vietnam.

Thus started the ghastly war with all of its terrible social ramifications. There was no conscientious investigation, no thoughtful debate, and no formal vote on a declaration of war. However, the CIA's drug business flourished, and heroin use by GIs became endemic, being available wherever GIs were to be found. Medical personnel estimated in 1971 that 10 to 15 percent of GIs were users; in 1973, a White House task force found that 34 percent of GIs back from Vietnam had "commonly used" heroin. To boot, the USA lost the war, so couldn't even say that the war's gains justified its many losses, the result of our intruding into the affairs of another country not threatening us, a direct violation of George Washington's wise advice.

6. The Israeli-Palestinian War
The Balfour Declaration (dated November 2, 1917) stated that:

> His Majesty's government views with favour the establishment in Palestine of a national home for the Jewish people, and will use their best endeavours to facilitate the achievement of this object, it being clearly understood that nothing shall be done which may prejudice the civil and religious rights of existing non-Jewish communities in Palestine, or the rights and political status enjoyed by Jews in any other country.

The British were then given a League of Nations mandate, dated July 24, 1922, to administer Palestine until such time as the Jewish homeland came into existence.

Britain, exhausted by World War II, and frustrated by the incipient conflict within their Palestinian Mandate, announced their desire to terminate the Mandate and place the question of Palestine before the United Nations, the now extant successor to the League of Nations.

On November 29, 1947, the UN General Assembly voted in favour of its Partition Plan, to take effect on the date of British withdrawal. Both the U.S. and the Soviet Union supported the resolution, but the five members of the Arab League who were then voting members voted against it. The Israeli state-in-formation joyfully accepted the plan, but it was rejected out of hand by Palestinian Arab leaders and by most of the Arab population, whose real estate was being co-opted. The Arab League then began looking for a military solution to the conflict.

Britain refused to help implement the plan, arguing that it was not acceptable to both sides, and announced its decision to terminate the Mandate by August 1, 1948. Some Jewish organizations also opposed the proposal. Irgun leader Menachem Begin announced: "The partition of the homeland is illegal. It will never be recognized. The Land of Israel will be restored to the people of Israel. All of it. And forever."

On May 14, 1948 the provisional Jewish government led by David Ben-Gurion declared independence and was recognized by the U.S., the USSR, and many other countries, but not by the surrounding Arab states. Many of the latter invaded Israel, and the war began, with no real peace to this very day (early 2011). When Britain left the scene on August 1, 1948, the Jewish provisional government declared the formation of the State of Israel. The partition plan required that the proposed states grant full civil rights to all people within their borders, but Israel was immediately seen as having no intention of complying with such conditions.

For about 30 years Israel was led by its Labor party, which pragmatically accepted the two-state partition, though it violated its terms by overrunning the West Bank and Gaza Strip. By 1977 an opposition party led by Menachem Begin came to power, evolving shortly into the Likud party. That party went beyond just the West Bank and the Gaza Strip to their much larger vision of "Eretz Israel." The extent of the desired expansion continues to be debated today by the several Israeli factions.

FOREIGN ISSUES

Israel Shahak, in his *Jewish History, Jewish Religion* (Ref. 9, pp. 9-11) defines the Likudists goal of Eretz Israel, (or Biblical Israel, or Greater Israel) as everything within the rough square starting at the Nile River near Cairo, eastward to include the northeast corner of Egypt, the Sinai Peninsula, a swath of Saudi Arabia, and the whole of Kuwait on the Persian Gulf, northward through Iraq to the Lake Van area in Turkey, westward to the Mediterranean coast, southward back along the coast to the Nile River, and down to Cairo. Also claimed is the island of Cyprus. The present-day countries impacted by this Likudist dream are Egypt, Saudi Arabia, Kuwait, Iraq, Turkey, Syria, Lebanon, Jordan, and, of course, Israel itself.

In addition to reclaiming the "Biblical Borders" granted by Jehovah himself, Shahak identifies a more modern imperialistic consideration for such expansion, voiced by Israeli general Shlomo Gazit:

Israel's main task… remains of crucial importance. The geographical location of Israel at the center of the Arab-Muslim Middle East predestines Israel to be a devoted guardian of stability in all the countries surrounding it. Its [role] is to protect the existing regimes, to prevent or halt the processes of radicalization, and to block the expansion of fundamentalist religious zealotry.

For this purpose Israel will prevent changes occurring beyond Israel's borders [which it] will regard as intolerable, to the point of feeling compelled to use all its military power for the sake of their prevention or eradication.

In other words, says Shahak, Israel aims at imposing hegemony over other Middle Eastern states. Middle Eastern leaders are fully aware of this mindset, and of the support given Israel by the U.S. It is no surprise that many of them hate us, not because they are jealous of our freedom, but because our policies will result in relieving them of whatever freedoms they presently enjoy.

Uncle Sam has boldly stepped into this hornet's nest to fix everything up and make everyone happy. We were conned into World War I and the Balfour Declaration, then into recognizing Israel after World War II, and now into supporting Israel's imperialistic objectives. We keep trying to make peace, but Israel clearly does not want peace. It wants supremacy, a goal that has not changed in at least 3000 years, and which our puny efforts are unlikely to change. Washington was right. Let's work on fixing up our own problems, staying out of religious wars, and letting other countries spend *their own* treasure on solving their own problems.

7. The First Iraq War

Iraq invaded Kuwait on August 2, 1990, and the U.S. massively came to Kuwait's aid with an aerial assault on January 16, 1991 and a ground assault on February 23, 1991. A cease-fire was declared on February 28, 1991.

The origin of European involvement in Kuwait came in January 1899, when the Kuwaiti ruler Mubarak al-Sabah ("Mubarak the Great") signed an agreement with the British giving Britain control of Kuwait's foreign policy. In return, Britain would guarantee Kuwait's national security and would also grant an annual subsidy of 15,000 Indian rupees to the Sabah family. A cozy relationship has existed between Britain and Kuwait ever since.

What motivated Britain? Oil hadn't yet been found in Kuwait. However, with the control of Kuwaiti foreign policy, Britain could and did deny Germany access from Baghdad to the Persian Gulf, making it impossible for them to complete the last link of their Baghdad to Berlin railroad. Access to the Gulf from Baghdad implies also the access via a sea route (read tankers) between Germany and the known Near East oil fields. (See Ref. 2, pp. 5-6.) Britain was then laying the groundwork for World War I, and their actions were in accord with their geopolitical agenda. (See Ref. 3, pp. 264-271.)

By the 1930's Kuwait was found to contain massive oil deposits. The Kuwaiti Oil Company was formed in 1934 as an equal partnership between the predecessors of BP and Chevron. The company was nationalized in 1975, though good relations were maintained between Kuwait and the former KOC owners, right up to the time of the First Iraq War.

Things did not go as well between Kuwait and Iraq. Kuwait had heavily funded Iraq's eight-year war with Iran, but when the war ended, Kuwait refused to forgive Iraq's war debt to Kuwait, perhaps $25 billion. More bad feeling followed when Kuwait increased its oil production by 40 percent, depressing oil prices, and severely cutting Iraq's oil profits. Iraq further accused Kuwait of slant drilling into an adjacent Iraqi oil field.

We turn now to Iraq history. After World War I, the Ottoman properties were distributed among the victors. The San Remo Resolution adopted on April 25, 1920 incorporated the Balfour Declaration of 1917. Britain received the League of Nations mandate for both Palestine and Iraq; and France got Syria, including the present-day Lebanon.

Significant middle eastern oil was discovered in the 1920's leading to nationalization of oil reserves by the countries so blessed. Iraqi attempts to do so in 1953 were repulsed by the West via the assassination of the Iraqi President, General Qassem, but were successful by President Saddam Hussein in 1972. Hussein was thereafter not popular with the Western Powers.

(Iran successfully nationalized their oil in 1953 under President Mossadegh, who was then ousted and replaced in a CIA coup by the Shah of Iran, thereafter popular for a time with the West, but certainly not with Iranians. He was in turn overthrown by the fundamentalist Ayatollah Khomeini, who had little interest in cooperating with the West.)

For reasons best known to himself, Hussein then attacked Iran. The U.S., not liking either of them, supplied military goods to both of them, including anthrax weaponry to Iraq, perhaps to let them demolish each other, which would certainly be consistent at least with the agenda of our "best ally," Israel. By the war's end, Iraq was $25 billion in debt to Kuwait, as noted above. Financially hurting, Hussein looked greedily across his southern border at the immensely profitable Kuwaiti oil fields, and recalled that Kuwait had 100 years earlier been a part of Iraq. The West, of course, wanted to protect that oil for their own uses, and, viewing Iraq's war preparations, laid their own plans to save Kuwait for themselves.

A few days before Iraq's invasion, the State Department's April Glaspie told Saddam that the U.S. took no position regarding arguments between Arab states. Saddam took that as a green light, and on August 2, 1990, he invaded Kuwait.

On August 7, the U.S. military was in Saudi Arabia, convincing the Saudis of the untruth that they were in imminent danger of an Iraqi invasion, and that they should let the U.S. establish bases in their country so that they could help Kuwait and protect Saudi Arabia. The Saudis accepted the offer, and within 24 hours the first of 500,000 American troops starting arriving in Saudi Arabia.

The U.S. pressured the UN to sanction the war, and they reluctantly did, on November 29, 1990, giving Saddam a deadline to remove his troops from Kuwait by January 15, 1991. On January 17, 1991, the U.S. began to bomb Baghdad. The bombing was not indiscriminate, but was specifically aimed at the civilian infrastructure. Dams, pumping stations, and filtration plants were wiped out, as were electric power stations, the transportation system, and the food chain from one end of the country to the other. Perhaps 150,000 to 200,000 people were killed, with thousands more to die indirectly in the months ahead. The U.S. proved that a country could be destroyed without a physical invasion.

On February 23, the U.S. sent its ground troops into Kuwait, meeting negligible resistance. Most of Saddam's army had never even entered Kuwait. On February 28 the U.S., having cleared Kuwait of any remaining Iraqi army, announced a cease-fire, and the war ended.

In summary, this section of Chapter 12 concerned with the First Iraq War has mentioned the following things that our U.S. political administration had done in violation of George Washington's admonition not to become enmeshed in other countries' internal affairs:

1. Ran the 1953 CIA coup against Iran's Pres. Mossadegh.
2. Armed both sides in the Iran-Iraq war, 1980-1988.
3. Encouraged the Kuwait-Iraq war, and supported Kuwait.
4. Lied to the Saudis about Iraq's intention to invade them.
5. Unnecessarily killed hundreds of thousands of Iraqis in support of a war between foreign countries over foreign oil rights, intensifying the middle eastern hatred of the United States.

8. The Afghan War
As described in Chapter 10, Russia invaded Afghanistan on Dec. 24, 1979. The U.S. and its CIA spent, through the ISI (Pakistani intelligence), some $40 billion, and Russia withdrew in 1989. Poppy production and the transport of opium to Pakistani heroin labs were overseen by the former guerilla fighter Gulbuddin Hekmatyar.

The State of Afghanistan was formed in April of 1992.Chaos reigned for a few years, with huge refugee traffic to Pakistan. The Taliban, supported by Pakistan and Saudi Arabia, was formed in 1994, won control of Kabul in September of 1996, and established the Islamic Emirate of Afghanistan. Then, joined by Osama bin Laden and his Al- Qaeda organization, it fought the State of Afghanistan and its Northern Alliance into the year 2001.

The fundamentalist religious elements of the Taliban were hard on the women, but they were also violently against the drug trade. Poppy planting was outlawed in November of 2000, resulting in a negligible crop in 2001, with the same projected for future years. Since Afghanistan had produced in 2000 about three-quarters of the world's opium, and even more than that in 1999, the big money moguls of the drug trade must have noted the outlawing of poppy farming with considerable concern.

About a year later, the 9/11/2001 events occurred. The U.S. blamed Osama bin Laden, and demanded that the Taliban turn him over. It didn't, and the U.S. started bombing Taliban and Al-Qaeda targets, and still is (as of early 2011). The Taliban was ejected from Kabul in December of 2001, and Hamid Karzai was soon installed as the Afghan president. Opium production is again bigger than ever, with a portion of the drug profits going to the Taliban to help finance its war against the Karzai regime. The CIA and Gulbuddin Hekmatyar are presumably still performing their designated roles, while the U.S. is visibly in bed with the corrupt Karzai, who also appears to be banking drug receipts. It looks an awful lot as if we're funding both sides of this Afghan War.

If George Washington became President of the United States tomorrow, we would be out of Afghanistan the day after tomorrow, and a big contingent of U.S. politicians and bankers would be on their way to trial for treason. Since that's not likely to happen, an alternative action is needed.

A Congress of Honest Constitutionalists should hold investigative hearings, not just aimed at the illegal drug activity by American officialdom in Afghanistan, but at the entirety of the whole fraudulent 9/11 affair. There are dozens of alternative media books and tapes presently available seeking the truth about what really happened. We won't go into all of that here, except to note one reference of our own: Ref. 4, p. 65, and the two references therein noted, repeated as References 6 and 7 on our References page.

All that the HC Congress needs to do to make a sea change in the history of our world is: (1) establish the Congress' own media, per Chapter

1 above, (2) out of the hundreds or perhaps thousands of persons who had pre-knowledge of the 9/11 events, or who were involved in the coverup, find two or three persons willing to break their silence and become a part of history, and (3) give those persons protection, immunity, and a public platform in a congressional hearing which will be electronically delivering the testimony directly to the public, rendering immaterial the coverage, if any, provided by the mainstream media.

Terminating the war, getting the right people impeached and jailed, and completing the other tasks described in the preceding chapters then become highly doable.

9. The Second Iraq War

On March 20, 2003, about 18 months after the 9/11 events and well into the Afghan War with poppy and heroin production blossoming nicely, G.W. Bush had the U.S. invade Iraq a second time, this time with a force of around 300,000 mostly American soldiers. In about a month, Baghdad fell and Bush publicly declared, "Mission Accomplished." However, the fighting went on for over seven more years, with President Obama announcing in February of 2009 that the "U.S. combat mission will end by August 31, 2010." With some residual fighting still going on, the last combat brigades did withdraw by that date, but left behind some 50,000 troops "to help train Iraqi security forces." In addition, the new U.S. embassy in Baghdad is the largest U.S. embassy in the world, with its size presently planned to be doubled, not suggestive of early permanent withdrawal.

The announced objectives of the conflict were to disempower Saddam Hussein (he was found, tried, and then executed on December 30, 2006), to find and eliminate any existing weapons of mass destruction, to obtain intelligence on militant networks, to secure Iraq's petroleum infrastructure, to provide humanitarian relief, and to help create a representative but compliant government as a model for other Middle East countries. In addition, as the war went on its justification was adjusted to include finding and expunging Al-Qaeda elements in Iraq, since Al-Qaeda was the source from which sprang the publicly identified terrorists who had (allegedly) executed the 9/11 affair.

In reality, the only objectives which mattered to the Neocon instigators of the Second Iraq War were (1) to get rid of Saddam Hussein, who was still blocking the oligarchs from their unimpeded exploitation of Iraqi oil, (2) to create an Iraqi government which would permit such exploitation (Iraq awarded some production contracts to international oil companies in June, 2009), and (3) though not an announced objective, to destroy one of the major obstacles blocking the way to the fulfillment of the Israeli dream of Eretz Israel, namely, a Near Eastern country with a strong central government opposed to Israel. The issues of destroying WMDs, of gaining intelligence about terrorists, of rebuilding infrastructure, providing humanitarian relief, and building model democratic nations were all grist for media propaganda aimed at the American public to convince it to accept the Neocons' destruction of Iraq.

George Washington would be appalled. If we want Iraqi oil, why not just offer to buy it from them if their oil is the cheapest or is otherwise our optimum source of supply? Alternatively, we could develop and use our own resources in Alaska (the North Slope) and the North Dakota area (the Bakken Formation). We should reject the establishment's aim of keeping us at war, in debt, and nearing national bankruptcy, all truly aimed at destroying the U.S. middle class and creating a One World Government a la George Orwell's *1984*. (See Ref. 2, pp. 120-130.)

10. Incipient Wars – Pakistan and Iran

The preceding nine U.S. involvements have been so successful for the oligarchs that it is to be expected that they will favor continuing down this path. If we wish to ever interrupt their program, we must keep our eyes peeled for clues concerning the next events being planned, and then do our best to obviate them.

Regarding Pakistan, that country is being criticized for helping the Taliban in neighboring Afghanistan and for providing a safe haven for its leaders. Pakistan has even undergone some drone bombings, complete with civilian casualties, explained away by the U.S. military as collateral damage stemming from their efforts to kill the Taliban insurgent leadership. These events could rationally be taken as the beginnings of a propaganda war on the U.S. psyche to get our public to accept a war against Pakistan.

The true motivation for such a war could be that Pakistan is the only Arab country with operational nuclear weapons, and as such is a major obstacle on Israel's road to Eretz Israel. From Israel's point of view, it would be highly desirable to persuade the U.S. to execute a regime change in Pakistan, with the "right" persons ending up in control. The goal would be to leave Israel the only Middle Eastern country having a nuclear arsenal, making Eretz Israel truly a rational possibility. The desirability of the world's avoiding such an outcome is obvious.

With respect to Iran, the propaganda drumbeat against its nuclear program has been in operation for many years, but the public is still aware that Iran has no nuclear weapons, and is having significant difficulty in attaining "success," probably defined by them as having enough weapons to prevent Israel from ever using theirs. Israel and the U.S. are reportedly engaged in the sabotage of Iran's enrichment facilities, and doing whatever else is available to them to slow down Iran's nuclear development.

Without an event producing a more overt threat, the situation is likely to continue simmering for a long time. If Israel and the U.S. could bring about yet another regime change in Iran to their own advantage, they could in short order stop Iran's nuclear development, destroy its nuclear facilities, and regain control of its oil as they did following Mossadegh's removal over 55 years ago. Israel would thereby gain a much freer hand in the Middle East, leaving only Pakistan obstructing its goal of attaining Eretz Israel.

George Washington would advise us to stop supporting Israel's war-making capabilities, be neutral toward Iran, and let the whole world know that the U.S. is terminating its military support of all Middle Eastern countries, will support no combatants in any future war between Israel and its neighbors, and will instead see to its own national security and encourage the rest of the world to do the same.

Chapter 13

Quit Oligarchy's Institutions

To facilitate the oligarchy's drive toward creating a One World Order which they will control, they have created a number of international organizations which we shall set about to separate ourselves from. (See Ref. 3, p. 352.) Accordingly, we propose that the following actions be taken as soon as an adequate Honest Constitutionalist Congress has been attained:

1. Terminate our membership in the United Nations and its several agencies, and eject the UN, its agencies, and its activities from the United States. The UN, created by the oligarchy after World War II as a replacement for the League of Nations, is generally heralded as a peace-keeping entity, whereas in reality its one most effective function is to sanction, or legitimize, the wars that are desired by the oligarchy, including such as the Korean War, the Vietnam War, the Yugoslav-Kosovo War, and the wars in Iraq and Afghanistan.

2. Terminate membership in the World Bank and the IMF, and recover US investments or deposits therein. The World Bank's charter is to advise and lend money to financially struggling countries; the IMF's job is to enforce measures in such countries to enable those World Bank loans to be repaid, through the application of austerity measures, payment via transfer of ownership of physical assets, etc. Ref. 8 contains an excellent description of the methodology, and Ref. 3, pp. 90-99, provides a quick summary. In one or two words, financial neophytes are suckered into borrowing money they can't rationally repay, and the oligarchs from that point on have control over the targeted country. In reality, the ploy consists of massive fraud, for which the instigators would in an honest world be incarcerated.

3. Terminate membership in the North American Free Trade Agreement (NAFTA) and the World Trade Organization

(WTO). NAFTA is the first step of consolidation by the oligarchy of the North American Union, conceived as a parallel in the North American hemisphere to the European Union across the ocean. It only dealt with economic issues, however, enabling the American public to be more easily conned into giving up hunks of American sovereignty. (An "agreement" doesn't have to be ratified by the U.S. Senate, and it was not.) The WTO does not, of course, guarantee "free trade," though that is commonly claimed by the establishment. It is, pure and simple, managed trade, with the managing done by international bureaucrats approved by the oligarchy. We should stick with the trade policies defined in Chapters 4 and 7 above, by which Congress remains in control of our trade policies.

4. Terminate the use of U.S. military forces to implement UN directives or other imperatives requiring a world military presence. NATO, the North Atlantic Treaty Organization, was created to serve as a military bulwark against the expansion of Communism. Following the collapse of the USSR, it morphed into a military agency largely in the service of the UN. We should certainly get out of NATO, and refrain from injecting our country into any other military adventures around the world that are not for our own defense, as we exhaustively argued in the previous chapter. The U.S. military should of course retain its own unique role of protecting and defending the U.S.A.

5. Revive and pass the "Bricker Amendment" to the Constitution, to provide that no treaty or other governmental agreement shall be deemed effective as internal law unless it could have been passed by valid, constitutional, congressional legislation. This will prevent international or foreign entities to which we may become connected by treaty or agreement from imposing upon us law which our own system would find unconstitutional, such as submitting our country to the findings of the UN's International Court of Justice. In 1954 the Bricker Amendment missed by one vote in the Senate being sent to the States for ratification. Today we are more in need of it than ever, and it should be reintroduced as soon as Honest Constitutionalism again reigns in Congress.

6. Terminate any governmental funding of Non-Governmental Organizations (NGOs) that are doing organizational work for the oligarchs around the world. There are many thousands of such international organizations, offering myriad job opportunities for persons willing to do the oligarchs' work. Many of them are linked to the work of the UN all around the world, and are assuredly linked to oligarchic goals. Our own government certainly should not be supporting them.

7. Strengthen and enforce the Logan Act, penalizing US private citizens or organizations for unauthorized negotiating with or lobbying foreign governmental officials on behalf of the United States, in order to bring about changes in provisions of US laws, treaties, or policies. The act was passed in 1799 at the behest of President Adams upon the effort of a Dr. George Logan to get France to release some American sailors the French had jailed. He was successful, but Adams saw it as interference with the processes of government. The law has rarely thereafter been applied, except as a warning to civilians to let government do its work. With the advent of thousands of American citizens involved with NGOs having highly questionable goals, strengthening and advertising the existence of the Logan Act might avoid a great deal of future grief.

Chapter 14

Create World Freedom Institute

Having terminated our UN membership in Chapter 13, we now embark on creating a new international organization, not having the goal of eventually controlling the world, but rather of spreading across the world the goals that the founders of the United States had in mind for their new country, namely, to protect the inalienable rights of its individual citizens to life, liberty, and the pursuit of happiness.

To that end, the U.S. should take the lead in creating a new international organization composed of member nations (a) whose citizens are already living under governmental charters which seek to guarantee the maintenance of their citizens' freedom, (b) that desire to join with other countries of that kind for the purpose of giving and gaining mutual help in strengthening those guarantees, and (c) that are admitted into the new organization by the sufferance of the existing members.

We shall call the new organization the International Freedom Organization (IFO), the primary attributes of which are:

1. Membership shall be limited to countries having a constitution, and a conforming government, whose primary goal is to guarantee the rights of its individual citizens to life, liberty, and the pursuit of happiness, with lesser goals assigned to the rights of any other political, social, or business entities in the nation.

2. Membership shall be granted, and may be rescinded, by vote of the existing membership, but only after whatever detailed examination of the applicant government and its governing officials may be deemed necessary by the IFO, including Truth Testing using the modern Voice Stress Analysis techniques described in Chapter 3 above.

3. The IFO charter shall be continually examined by the IFO membership for possible improvements, with agreed-upon changes submitted to member countries for ratification or other

action, including abdication of membership.

4. Knowledge shall be shared of mechanisms and policies (such as protective tariffs) which promote national security, independence, economic growth, and citizen well-being.

5. Mechanisms shall be developed for negotiating proposed solutions to any significant disagreements among members, such solutions to be returned to member countries for ratification and/or other action.

6. A standard shall be raised demonstrating to non-member governments and populations how well the fundamental interests of a country's citizens can be served by patterning their governmental organization after those of IFO members.

7. Advice and help shall be offered to non-member nations concerning changes which would have to be made in a country's governing institutions in order for that country to become eligible for membership.

References

1. *Let's Fix America!*, ABJ, 1994, www.abjpress.com

2. *How the World Really Works*, ABJ, 1996, abjpress.com

3. *Secrecy or Freedom?*, ABJ, 2001, abjpress.com

4. *Restoring Political Honesty*, ABJ, 2006, abjpress.com

5. http://www.humanevents.com/article.php?id=13863

6. *Pentagate*, Thierry Meyssan, 2002, Amazon.com

7. *9/11 Synthetic Terror*, Webster Tarpley, 2005, Amazon.com

8. *Creature from Jekyll Island*, G.E. Griffin, 1994, Amazon.com

9. *Jewish History, Jewish Religion*, Israel Shahak, 1994, Amazon.com

Several paragraphs from the Ref. 5 article follow. In the article, "MEChA" is an acronym for Movimiento Estudiantil Chicano de Aztlan, or Chicano Student Movement of Aztlan.

MEChA isn't at all shy about their goals, or their views of other races. Their founding principles are contained in these words in "El Plan Espiritual de Aztlan" (The Spiritual Plan for Aztlan):

"In the spirit of a new people that is conscious not only of its proud historical heritage but also of the brutal gringo invasion of our territories, we, the Chicano inhabitants and civilizers of the northern land of Aztlan from whence came our forefathers, reclaiming the land of their birth and consecrating the determination of our people of the sun, declare that the call of our blood is our power, our responsibility, and our inevitable destiny. ... Aztlan belongs to those who plant the seeds, water the fields, and gather the crops and not to the foreign Europeans. ... We are a bronze people with a bronze culture. Before the world, before all of North America, before all our brothers in the bronze continent, we are a nation, we are a union of free pueblos, we are Aztlan. For La Raza todo. Fuera de La Raza nada."

That closing two-sentence motto is chilling to everyone who values equal rights for all. It says, "For The Race everything. Outside The Race, nothing."

MEChA and the La Raza movement teach that Colorado, California, Arizona, Texas, Utah, New Mexico, Oregon, and parts of Washington State make up an area known as "Aztlan" -- a fictional ancestral homeland of the Aztecs before Europeans arrived in North America. As such, it belongs to the followers of MEChA. These are all areas America should surrender to "La Raza" once enough immigrants, legal or illegal, enter to claim a majority, as in Los Angeles. The current borders of the United States will simply be extinguished.

This plan is what is referred to as the "Reconquista" or reconquest, of the Western U.S.

End

Ordering Information

Ordering Information: (prices do not include shipping costs)

Let's Fix America!..$15

How the World REALLY Works $15

Secrecy or Freedom? $15

Restoring Political Honesty $15

Restoring American Freedom...$15

Get all five books above as a set for $60.

Mix and match: Any five books above for $60

Prices do not include S&H. Inside the U.S. add: $3 S&H on orders up to $35; $5 S&H on orders from $35.01 to $50; $7 S&H on orders from $50.01 to $75; and $10 S&H on orders over $75—no matter the size. Outside U.S. double these charges.

Send check or money order to American Free Press, 645 Pennsylvania Avenue SE, #100, Washington, D.C. 20003. Call AFP toll free at 1-888-699-6397 to charge to Visa, MasterCard, AmEx or Discover. You can also order online at americanfreepress.net, amazon.com or abjpress.com.

Low-cost case lots are also available for those wishing to undertake bulk distribution. Please call American Free Press at 202-547-5585 for bulk distribution prices.

Note that carte blanche permission has been granted, and is here restated, to reproduce these books in whole or part in order to further their distribution.

For author's reviews of these books, see www.abjpress.com.